...BUT
GRACE
IS ENOUGH

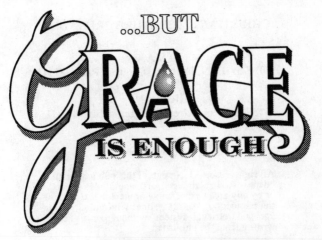

...BUT GRACE IS ENOUGH

KEN RADKE

CHRISTIAN • LITERATURE • CRUSADE
Fort Washington, Pennsylvania 19034

CHRISTIAN LITERATURE CRUSADE

U.S.A.
P.O. Box 1449, Fort Washington, PA 19034

BRITAIN
51 The Dean, Alresford, Hants SO24 9BJ

ISBN 0-87508-459-1

Printed in Colombia

Scripture quotations from:
The *New American Standard Bible*, © 1960, 1962, 1963, 1968, 1971,
   1972, 1973, 1975, 1977 by The Lockman Foundation, unless
   otherwise indicated. Used by permission.
The *Holy Bible, New International Version (NIV)*. Copyright © 1973,
   1978, International Bible Society.
The *King James Version of the Bible (KJV)*.
The *New King James Bible — New Testament (NKJV)*. Copyright ©
   1979, 1982, Thomas Nelson, Inc., Publishers.

Other quoted material is acknowledged in the Notes at the back of the book.

IMPRESO EN COLOMBIA

BUENA SEMILLA
Apartado 29724
Bogotá, Colombia

To My Wife, Sue
who is God's gift of grace to me.

My Thanks To
my wife for encouraging me to write,
and to Barbara Krismanth for her
labor of love in typing and retyping
the manuscript; also to Harold and
Joy Geiss for researching Scripture
references and proofreading.

To run and work the law commands,
　　Yet gives me neither feet nor hands;
But better news the gospel brings:
　　It bids me fly, and gives me wings.[1]

TABLE OF CONTENTS

FOREWORD

Man was so engineered by God that the presence of the Creator in the creature is indispensable to his humanity. Christ in the Christian puts God back into the man, to be in him the Origin of His own image, the Source of His own activity, the Dynamic of His own demands and the exclusive Cause of His own effect! Only God is to be congratulated!

The "fruits of righteousness" are by Jesus Christ (Philippians 1:11), and He alone can be in us the source of all that goodness of which the Father alone was the source in Him. The moral law, etched with the finger of God on tables of stone and given to Moses on Mount Sinai, describes to perfection the righteousness that derives from the life of God; but the law cannot restore to man the life of God from which that righteousness derives. The law, exposing man's moral bankruptcy, is our schoolmaster to bring us to Christ, that in Him we might receive that life, God's life, that restores our moral competence.

In the following pages, Ken Radke describes the unhappy lot of those who with no little sincerity seek in vain to achieve *for* Christ what He alone can *be* in us—the righteousness of God. They fight a battle already lost, instead of celebrating a victory already won! The birthright of the redeemed is to "reign in life by one, Jesus Christ," to be "more than conquerors through Him that loved us," for "the law of the Spirit of Life in Christ Jesus has set us free from the law of sin and death."

The author applies this principle of Christ's divine indwelling in several practical ways, and although he does not ask his readers to agree with him in everything he says, especially in the controversial matter of physical healing, he does insist, and rightly so, that the Lord Jesus Christ as God in us must be the Author of all that we do and are, in life or death, in sickness or in health, in poverty or in wealth. Christ, as God's ultimate provision for all our needs, must be the only explanation for our lives.

All there is of Christ in all there is of you—you cannot have more and you need never enjoy less! That is the abundance of grace that God bestows upon us in the Person of His dear Son, the One in whom dwells all the fullness of the Godhead bodily and in whom we are complete.

I am sure that you who read these pages will be greatly encouraged to enter more fully into your inheritance in Christ, by allowing Him to have His full inheritance in you. Delivered from the frustration and futility of your own self-effort in attempting to accomplish for Christ what He alone can accomplish in you, at last you will know for yourself what John meant when he wrote, "if the Son shall set you free, you will be FREE INDEED!"

W. Ian Thomas

INTRODUCTION

Have you ever felt the need for a second chance? Have you ever wanted to erase the last several days and start over with a clean slate? If so, what you are really longing for is grace. It's more than a theological concept. It's the most powerful life-changing force in the world today.

The word itself has a beautiful ring about it: GRACE! Hymns and poems come to mind as we try to grasp its significance. "Amazing grace, how sweet the sound. . . . Wonderful grace of Jesus. . . . Marvelous grace of our loving Lord, Grace that exceeds our sin and our guilt."

This concept of grace is obviously important to the writers of Scripture. The word appears over 150 times in the Bible. Paul begins and ends almost every letter with "The grace of our Lord Jesus be with you." The last verse of the entire Bible is about grace. Yet for many, this beautiful word has lost its meaning. What was a powerful and life-changing force in the first century has now become a vague religious sentiment. Our need is to return to the radical New Testament definition of grace and to discover its potential for profound impact on our daily living. To be "saved by grace" is just the beginning of the power it can release in our lives.

The book of Hebrews speaks of two mountains standing side by side. The first is Mt. Sinai and it represents the law. Gathered around it are all those fearful souls of the judged and condemned. The second mountain is Mt. Zion, and it represents the gospel. Gathered upon it is a joyful assembly of those whose spirits have been made perfect by Christ's blood. One mountain does not have a mean God and the other a friendly one—it's the same holy Judge who sits on both. The difference is the Mediator of the Covenant. Jesus with His grace is upon Mt. Zion, and that's the reason for all the rejoicing. The purpose of this book is to help people move from the mountain of the law, with its unattainable perfectionism, over to the mountain where Jesus dwells. The writer to the Hebrews says, "For you have not come to" the mountain of the law, "but you have come to Mt. Zion," the mountain of the gospel of grace (Hebrews 12:18,22). Our need is to stay on the gospel mountain.

This is not a thorough doctrinal study of grace for the theology student. Rather it is a practical guide with simple illustrations for the average person. I pray that no one will be hurt by this book and that none of its teachings will be misapplied— for any truth can be taken to an extreme. It is my hope, rather, that all who read it will be encouraged to set their hope fully on the grace that is given to them.

How marvelous, infinite, matchless is the grace of our loving God!

CHAPTER 1

THE GOOD SHIP GRACE

If you study the teaching techniques of Jesus, you will find that He often used parables and stories to get His message across. I would like to do the same. I shall start with the tale of a newly converted young woman, and then tell a parable about an overconfident swimmer—both of whom get into some dangerous waters. First, the girl's story.

After some confidence-shattering experiences—we won't go into her background—Sally came to faith in Christ. It became the greatest joy of her life to realize that now she was saved—not by good works, but by the perfect sacrifice of Christ and the wonderful grace of God. Life took on a whole new meaning, the Bible became a pleasure to read, and she was confident that her new Friend would never forsake her.

Sally joined a church and began to get involved. She loved the spiritual feeding she received from the pastor's Bible messages. She joined a Sunday School class and began to sing in the choir. Surrounded by loving fellow-Christians, she began to grow. But as time went on, things did not stay the same. Her initial feelings of forgiveness and acceptance with God began to weaken. Many practices that were initially spontaneous had to be maintained now by rigorous duty and discipline. Doubts about her acceptance by God began to creep into her mind. "Could God actually be *that* loving?" she asked herself.

At the same time that these changes were taking place in Sally, changes were also taking place in many of her new Christian friends. Some began to emphasize the need to be more spiritual and many devoted themselves to fasting, various forms of self-denial, and strict attendance at all the meetings. Sally conformed to all of this for several reasons. She desired to be in the inner ring, and she also desired a greater closeness to God. Her spiritual friends, she noticed, seemed to frown on some of her personal practices, so she yielded to their dictates. She spoke their vocabulary, looked down on what they looked down upon, laughed at what they laughed at, dressed the way they dressed, and in general "fit in." But she felt no closer to God.

So Sally continued to increase her personal disciplines. The more she sensed a need for acceptance, the more she would pray, confess, give, fast, work, attend, and conform. She was now very much a part of the inner ring—and yet had never felt so distant from God. Her family life was beginning to suffer as she attended meeting after meeting. Being "spiritual" had totally exhausted her and brought a subtle new philosophy into her subconscious. It was as if she and her friends believed in a God who said, "Whatever you don't like to do, that's exactly what I want you to be doing. And if you don't do it *perfectly*, then I won't accept you."

Sally was now plagued by guilt concerning these shortcomings and failures. She knew she was not living up to the standards of spirituality that her religious subculture strove for. She felt like a hypocrite—though she tried to live by her friends' convictions, yet she felt condemned by their example . . . as one "not living the Christian life." The inner messages she seemed to be hearing said, "You blew it! You're inadequate. You'll never measure up. There is no hope for you; no second chance. You might as well accept the fact that you're not good enough, and therefore are condemned." At this point, Sally realized she had actually been happier *before* she became a Christian than she was now with all her religiosity and seeming spirituality.

I raise the question, What happened to Sally? Where did all of her joy go? I believe the Apostle Paul has the answer. He wrote a letter to a whole group of Sallys, and it's called the Book of Galatians. Let me paraphrase its message: "Oh foolish Sally! Who tricked you into turning away from God's grace, and led you back to the law? Why are you trying to become an evangelical clone? Do you remember the perfect acceptance you had with

God the day you received Christ? You started with faith—so why are you now returning to works? At your conversion the Son of God came to live inside of the unique person that is YOU. So please, get back to the joy and spontaneity of resting in the unbreakable promises of God. With love, the Apostle Paul."

We now leave Sally and turn our attention to the young swimmer I spoke of at the beginning of the chapter. It's another way of looking at the same problem.

Barry had vastly overestimated his swimming ability. As he approached the water he noticed a red flag waving ominously from the lifeguard's empty chair; grains of sand stung his skin as gusts of wind whipped his hair in every direction. But he marched out confidently into the ocean surf anyway and began to swim. His goal—a lush island on the horizon. Soon he was moving at a steady pace . . . with the shore becoming more and more distant behind him. He covered the first several miles with ease, and felt a great sense of pride in his ability. But as the hours wore on, Barry began to tire. His legs felt like great weights and it was becoming more difficult to lift his arms.

At the same time Barry was growing weary, the sea was beginning to show its strength. The waves begin to lift him up and then crash him down. Now he couldn't keep his head above water. One wave after another crashed over him, and his confidence ebbed. Now he knew he was drowning in the violence of the storm, helpless to save himself. He realized the foolishness of his self-confidence. As he sank under the waves, he gave a faint cry for help.

Suddenly Barry felt strong arms reaching under his arms and around his chest. He was being lifted out of certain death and up into a large, beautiful sailing ship which had mysteriously appeared on the scene. As he sat in the dry security of the great vessel, he was overwhelmed with feelings of gratefulness. His life had been saved! Soon he felt his strength returning, and he began to walk about the craft. Around him he observed many others safely within the ship, working happily on the sails and lines. They seemed to have a certain restfulness as they labored for the Captain. No one was passive or idle, and yet all appeared to be relaxed and confident. It was a joyful atmosphere.

But now the story takes a strange new twist. Barry wanders over to the edge of the ship and peers over the rail. It's almost as if he is listening to some distant voice from the sea calling to him. Suddenly we observe him climbing onto the rail and diving back into the raging waters. His self-confidence is again asserting itself. Within a few moments he is gulping gallons of the sea and barely keeping his head above water. But he sees a little boat near him and struggles over to it. He drags himself into it—and is immediately handed a can by a weary man and told to start bailing. This boat is obviously sinking and about to take its toil-worn crew to the bottom of the sea. As Barry struggles and exhausts himself trying to stay afloat, he remembers the great ship and the man who had saved him. Why did he ever leave that ship? What made him think he could fare any better in the waves the second time? Could he ever get back to the safety of that first ship?

This little parable tells us about the working of law and grace. The law's call to perfection crashes against us like one wave after another. We are all like that swimmer, helpless to save ourselves by our own feeble efforts. Paul tells us that "by the works of the Law no flesh will be justified" (Romans 3:20). Over and over again these waves crash against us, dashing all hope of eternal life. The swimmer's guilt and foolishness were acknowledged when he realized that he deserved to die. His faith was expressed when he cried out for deliverance from the threatening storm—a rescue from outside of his own resources. The law can bring a person to the point of overwhelming despair; and it is at this place of helplessness that true faith springs to life. Onto this scene comes the first rescue craft, the good ship *Grace*.

Christ is the Captain of this great ship. He once swam those waters perfectly, then gave His life sacrificially, and now He lives to rescue helpless swimmers. Anyone who puts his faith in Him will be brought into the ship (Romans 3:22–24). But there is more here than merely being saved. There is *life*, with the Captain, riding on top of the waves and passing safely through the storm. Trusting in

Christ's cross is the only way to face *death* successfully; trusting in His resurrection is the only way to face *life* successfully.

Barry returned to the raging waters of the law, though, and went back to depending upon his own self-effort to keep afloat. There is this tendency within each of us, to hear the call of self-sufficiency and go back to the law's hopeless system. Soon the undertow of failure will begin to pull its victims down. But Barry discovered a second "rescue boat." It was legalism's leaky boat, a sinking craft, itself doomed to destruction. Religion is a poor replacement for relationship. On board that boat there was nothing better than the exhausting effort of the self-life, each person directed toward saving "number one." In contrast to this was the joyful work being done by those on board the good ship *Grace*. No one was passive there, but the work was not for self. They were all trusting in a ship that could keep them saved, and obeying the Captain out of love and gratitude.

Picture the vast churning seas with the wind driving the waves. There is only one ship available and equipped to save the people who are perishing there, and it is called *Grace*. This ship appears on the horizon of each person's life. "The grace of God that brings salvation to all men" (Titus 2:11 *NIV*). It is the only escape. Have you gotten on board yet? If not, then cry out to Christ by asking Him into your life and He will reach down and pull you into the ship. You will be "saved by grace" the moment you pray that prayer. It will be by none of your efforts, but all of His cross (Ephesians 2:8–9).

But suppose you have already been saved. The question I would like to ask you is, Which boat are you living in, legalism's leaking boat or Christ's good ship *Grace*? Jesus is the Captain of our salvation and the only one qualified to pilot us through life's storms. Are you sticking close to your Captain and letting Him be the Navigator of your life? If you will stay on board His ship, resting in His promises and following His commands, you will find life to be an exciting adventure on top of the waves rather than underneath them. Christ and His grace will help you reach your destination.

The rest of this book is written to all those people who may be in the wrong boat. It's written to the Barrys who sometimes become foolishly overconfident and to the Sallys who have become exhausted. It's written to contribute in some way to converting fearful and weary swimmers into happy and confident sailors. The ship is strong and secure. The Captain is wise and alert. So let's begin our journey on the good ship *Grace*.

CHAPTER 2

A DANGEROUS DOCTRINE?

Whenever the full extent of God's amazing grace is explained and applied, some people react with alarm. They see it as a swing too far in the direction of God's mercy and love. They become nervous and hold more tightly to their man-made rules and regulations. They see the grace of God as weak, but the discipline of man as strong. In fear that they might fall into license to sin (somewhere over on the "far left") they swing all the way over to the "far right" of legalism. They have forgotten that the center position of *liberty* is the true balance produced by grace. *Legalism is no answer to license*.

But there *are* dangers to be avoided when discussing grace. Some fears are understandable. Grace is not a dangerous doctrine . . . but men will sometimes apply it in dangerous ways. Perhaps you have known a Christian who was living sexually with his girl friend. When you challenged him with the teaching of Christ, he justified himself by saying, "It's not all that bad! And even if it is wrong, God is forgiving. After all, we are living under grace and not under law." This perversion is nothing new. Jude tells us that in his day there were those who perverted the grace of God into a license to commit immorality (Jude 4). Since the first century and before, people have been twisting God's grace to indulge themselves. But Paul doesn't back away from grace because some twist it.

A similar false premise is discussed by Paul in Romans: The greater the sin, the brighter shines forth grace in its brilliance. From this idea some wrongly conclude, "Great! I'll go ahead and commit lots of sin and then God will be able to demonstrate lots of grace. What a deal!" But Paul's reaction to this argument is swift and forceful. With strong indignation he counters with "God forbid!" (Romans 6:2 KJV). In moral outrage he explains that if we died to sin, it's unthinkable to continue indulging in it. True grace will never lead a man to more sin but rather to a fuller repentance. To emphasize the moral demands of the gospel is not *legalism*, but the plain teaching of Christ. If the spirit of holiness comes into my life through grace, He certainly won't live in an unholy way inside of me! If Jesus is the Truth, He won't use my lips to tell lies! If the gracious Father is a God of love, His presence won't make me unloving!

Then there are those who see grace as putting too much emphasis upon God's sovereignty and not enough upon man's responsibility. They see grace as a wimpy doctrine and quite feeble without a large dose of man's rules, man's efforts, and man's discipline. But the grace of Christ is far more than mere "unmerited favor." It is also unmerited *strength* which enables a person to live a far godlier life than the law could ever produce. Grace is no wimp! Paul told Timothy to "be strong in grace" (2 Timothy 2:1).

Another misapplication of grace is to see it as an anti-legalism system that permits one to ignore the moral commands of Scripture. Zealots may take grace and the indwelling-Christ doctrine to such an extreme that obedience is actually looked down upon. One group of "liberated Christians" I knew started a community supposedly based on grace. A committed Christian friend of mine moved into their community, but soon felt great tension. She discovered that these people were praying that she be "liberated" from her consistent practice of praying and reading her Bible each day! They wanted only to run around all day "being themselves" ...and assuming they had Christ's presence, with no reference to Christ's teachings. Surely this is an abuse of grace; there is nothing wrong with getting up in the morning, reading your Bible, and then doing what it says. *Obedience* is not legalism.

Grace is not a dangerous doctrine . It does *not* lead to moral irresponsibility or lazy passivity or disobedience. Rather, it is a strong, vibrant, and holy truth that will lead to a successful and fulfilling life! Contrary to some teaching, we are not saved by grace and then sanctified by the law. God's grace is both essential and central in winning every battle of life. We are *saved* by grace, *sanctified* by grace, and some day we will even be *glorified* by the grace of Christ. Don't be afraid of grace. Fear only that somehow you might miss the full scope of its power in your life.

The burden of Paul's letter to the Galatians is that once you're saved by grace, you cannot go back to the law for your strength. He expresses astonishment that those who were called to the grace of Christ and the life of faith have now turned to a different gospel, a religion of works, law, and flesh. For Paul, the real danger was not grace but legalism; it is that constant tendency in all of us to revert back to a system from which God has liberated us. So far from being a dangerous doctrine, grace is the only spiritually safe place to live. All else is sinking sand.

Legalism is dangerous! It gives man a false confidence in himself and his rule-keeping. All who rely upon it find themselves back under the curse. As John White has so clearly observed, man's answer to his sin is something *he* does. But God's answer to man's sin is the death of His Son![1] To miss this great truth is a failure to comprehend what is at the heart of the Christian message and to exchange the promise for the curse.

Phariseeism is dangerous! To focus on mini-ethics and spend all your days nit-picking, judging, and condemning your brothers is not the life

Jesus called us to. In fact, the Pharisees were the one group Jesus attacked with zeal. He had no stomach for their pettiness, hypocrisy, self-right-eousness, and judgment of others. To focus life around "separating oneself from the less spiritual" was and is a dangerous deviation from the life of love that grace opens up. No, do not fear the grace of God. What is dangerous is *not* God's unde-served goodness operating in us . . . but rather man's self-made religion, which drags us back to a bankrupt system.

Although there is a tendency in people to twist this beautiful doctrine into something ugly, the real danger is to ignore grace entirely. All of us face struggles and storms in our lives, and grace is God's way to get us through. The most dangerous thing a man can do in life is to face a storm without Jesus and His grace. Consider the situation several men found themselves in while sailing across a lake.

A tiny rip began to enlarge in the sail of the small boat. Soon the tearing sound was joined by the noise of water sloshing back and forth over the feet of the weary sailors. They were caught in a fierce gale! The creaking and groaning of the hull under the strain added to this cacophony of catastrophe. A look of desperation settled onto their faces as the rain and the driving spray lashed relentlessly against their every effort. The utter blackness of the night shrouded all hope of their ever seeing land again. They began to suspect that this battle with the elements might be the last effort of their young lives.

But suddenly a strange phenomenon occurs! At first only a few saw it. Then all twelve of them began to stare through the blackness at the dim figure approaching the boat. Were they losing their minds? Had the storm created an illusion? Or was this a trick the mind plays on a person who's about to change worlds? Their desperation turned to terror as the ghost-like figure moved one step at a time over the top of the churning water. The oars hung limp in their hands; their struggle with the storm was temporarily forgotten. Through the roar of the wind their ears heard the familiar voice of Jesus identifying Himself and issuing the unbelievable command to *put away their fear!* They had seen blind eyes healed; leprosy miraculously cured; demons instantly removed from hopeless lives. They had even witnessed the impossible feeding of 5,000 hungry people. But never had *their own* need been so great, never had their own personal desperation been so *intense*. Now, here was their Teacher, oblivious to the laws of gravity, and unaffected by the powers about to destroy them.

The final phase in the eyewitness account of this experience hints at a broader application to all of life. "They were willing therefore to receive Him into the boat; and immediately the boat was at the land to which they were going" (John 6:21). With Jesus in the boat *you'll reach the goal*. With Jesus in the boat you'll overcome the storm! With Jesus in the boat you'll conquer fear. If Jesus is in your boat, you're going to make it!

The storms of life strike everyone at one time or another. We know they're part of the weather of life; and yet it's always a shock to see them coming. Often the storm hits us from multiple angles. It would be bad enough just to have some water in the boat. But the darkness, the wind, the rain, and the shredded sails conspire to destroy us. That's the way it is with storms. They always take us by surprise and find us off guard and unprepared. They often hit from multiple angles, leaving us frustrated and despondent.

This book is about learning to sail those storms. It's a sailors' manual on the value of letting Jesus into the boat at our point of need. It's a chart for some of the rough seas we may have to sail through. But primarily, it's an encouragement to believe that whatever problems or struggles we may have to face, Jesus Christ and His astounding grace will be able to carry us through.

CHAPTER 3

THE TYRANNY OF THE LAW

God is wealthy in His abundant grace. In Him there is no stinginess as He showers the riches of His grace upon us. We are told in John 1 that Christ is filled to overflowing with grace, and that out of this fullness of grace each of us has received one blessing of grace piled on another and another. But how do we get in touch with all these blessings?

The answer is by first encountering the law. God's law is the opposite of God's grace. We first must understand law; only then can we comprehend grace. To appreciate grace, we must face law; to experience grace, we must first encounter law. It is not enough to take a passing glance at law, bounce off it, and ricochet over to grace. We must go through the law and feel the full weight of its burden before we will truly appreciate the grace of God.

The law was given the unpleasant task of revealing sin to people. "I would not have come to know sin except through the Law" (Romans 7:7). It's like an x-ray machine in the hospital. It shows us what's there and labels it. It gives us the bad news about our condition. If you ask the man on the street what the purpose of the Ten Commandments is, he'd likely say, "To make us good." But the exact opposite is the case. Their purpose is to show us how bad we really are. The law is only doing its job, so don't get mad at it! We shouldn't get mad at the policeman for giving us a speeding ticket or the dentist for telling us of our cavities. We shouldn't get mad at the banker for informing us that we're overdrawn or the bathroom scale for telling us we're overweight. The law is simply telling us the painful truth about ourselves, like the bathroom mirror we look into each morning upon getting out of bed. Some mornings that can be pretty bad news! The problem is not with the law. It is holy and righteous and good. The problem is inside of us.

But the law goes further than simply revealing sin; it actually provokes it. "But when the commandment came, sin became alive, and I died" (Romans 7:9). If you placed a sign in front of your picture window saying "Don't throw stones," you can be sure the rule itself would decrease the life of your window. Someone would take up the challenge. Human nature is just that way when it comes to keeping rules. So the law reveals, provokes and, finally, condemns sin. It's like the flag a football referee drops on the field for a holding penalty. It condemns and punishes the illegal action of the player.

What is it like to meet up with this tyrant called Law? You can compare it to meeting a giant on the street. He towers over you and carries a huge club in his hand. There is no escape. You must meet him. So you try to make the best of it and politely say hello to the giant. Immediately he lifts his club and strikes you on the head, sending you crashing to the ground. The shock has jarred your mind and you suddenly remember all the sin you've committed and all the mistakes you've made. So you struggle to your feet and tell Law that you know you've sinned, but you remind him that you've done lots of good things. The giant coldly responds with, "The soul that sins must die!" and he strikes you again on the head. You struggle to your feet a second time and ask Law for a second chance. "With me there is no second chance!" replies the giant as he strikes you on the head again. Now half dead, you pull yourself up to your knees and plead for mercy. "I show no mercy!" the giant responds, and dashes you to the ground one more time.

In hopeless despair, you begin to crawl down the street until you see a Man of Great Compassion walking past. You cry out for mercy and He reaches down with nail-pierced hands and touches your head. Instantly your strength and health are restored, and a clean, forgiven feeling sweeps through your conscience. After thanking the Man of Compassion, you tell Him all about the terrible giant called Law, and what a wicked enemy he is. But the Man of Compassion corrects you. "No, he is not evil; he's a friend. In fact, I sent him. If you hadn't met him first, you would never have realized your need to come to Me."

This is a parable of the gospel. Every person who has become a true Christian has first met the law and recognized his own sinfulness. That conviction of guilt was the very thing that led us to accept Christ into our lives and trust in His sacrifice on the cross. All pride is destroyed as we recognize along with Paul that it is "by grace you have been saved through faith; and that not of yourselves, it is the gift of God; not as a result of works, that no one should boast" (Ephesians 2:8–9).

Someone has compared the Christian life to a cup of hot water and a tea bag. There is a sense in which the water is neutral. If you place the tea bag in the hot water, it will take on the flavor and aroma of the tea leaves. The water will become a means of expressing and communicating what's in the tea bag. Christ is like the tea bag and we are the hot water. You could also put a deadly poison in the cup . . . and then the water would be contaminated by it. In like manner we can be expressions either of the beauty of Christ or of the deadly poison of our sin nature.

One of the most amazing verses in all the Bible is Galatians 2:20. "I have been crucified with Christ; and it is no longer I who live, but Christ lives in me; and the life which I now live in the flesh I live by faith in the Son of God, who loved me, and delivered Himself up for me." I understand this to mean that the key to real living is twofold. First, my sinful nature (not the true me) has been crucified with Christ. The evil, selfish part of me is now powerless, and I must continually "reckon" or consider it to be so. I must take up the cross daily. The cross is my identification with Christ's death, the negative side of righteousness. Second, my renewed nature (the true me) is indwelt and united with the resurrected Christ. I can be the unique person He created me to be—with all my unique tendencies and interests. By faith Christ will live within and express Himself through that "me." This is identification with Christ's resurrection and represents the positive side of righteousness.

Following that amazing verse is another fascinating statement. "I do not nullify the grace of God; for if righteousness comes through the Law, then Christ died needlessly" (Galatians 2:21). What this means is that if the law could cause a person to become a Christian and then live a righteous life, the sacrifice of Christ on the cross was unneeded, without purpose, and totally vain. Law cannot save, and its cousin Legalism can't sanctify. A non-Christian trying to get to heaven by means of the law and a Christian trying to be righteous by means of legalism—both are rejecting and nullifying God's grace. Paul is saying, "Don't exchange the beautiful union you have with your Compassionate Friend (Christ's grace) to go back under the tyranny of the great Giant (law)." The law of God is holy and good, but only useful in that it drives us to Christ, who then writes those principles of holiness and goodness upon our hearts.

Ian Thomas has commented that Moses gave the children of Israel the law without the land. But Joshua gave them the land in which to practice the law.[1] The lawgiver Moses was unable to lead them into the promised land. It is the same today. The law will never lead us into the place of spiritual fulfillment and fruitfulness. But our Divine Joshua, the Lord Jesus Christ, is able through His grace to give us the promised land in which to practice the law. The law came through Moses but grace and truth are from Jesus.

But there are some who would push the analogy too far, and not only contrast law with grace but actually pit them against each other. We should never go to this extreme of making friends into enemies. To do this is to become anti-law, which leads to a person throwing out the moral standards of God. Rather than put down law, we are to exalt grace into the place of centrality in our lives. When we do this, law will find its proper place. Under the new covenant, God's law is written on our hearts. No longer is it an external threat hanging over our heads but an internal motivation pulsating within our hearts. Under grace we don't throw law out the window but fulfill it in the deepest part of our being. Under grace, men will discover the true way to love people, maintain sexual purity, share rather than steal, speak truthfully and, in short, fulfill God's moral demands. Our Divine Joshua will lead us into the land of promise where we will practice the law of God. This is God's plan and provision through grace.

We might summarize a person's journey in relation to the law in the following way. First, we live in "I'm-a-pretty-good-guy" land. Life is blissfully self-confident until we meet Giant Law. He ushers us into "I'm-a-terrible-sinner" swamp. We escape this bog through conversion to Christ, who puts our feet on "I'm-a-new-person" rock. But alas, the enemy Legalism tries to lure us into "I'll-never-measure-up" marsh. We may spend years in this marsh thinking it's the normal Christian life. It is here we must experience a *second* self-exposure and move to the higher ground of "Christ-is-my-life" mountain.

The law plays a part in both these exposures of the self, the first leading to justification and the second to sanctification. Martin Luther said, "The law showeth unto them their sin that by the knowledge thereof, they may be humbled, terrified, bruised, and broken, and by this means may be driven to seek grace."[2] The only ones who really seek grace are those who have encountered the law in all of its strength. Law wounds a non-Christian and he accepts Christ. Law wounds a Christian more deeply and he begins truly to trust Christ and rely on His grace. Finally, with life now based on the undeserving goodness of God (grace), the fearful and terrifying Giant is melted into the ink of the loving character of Christ and inscribed on the heart. The Giant has been conquered by grace.

In each of the following chapters, we shall look at a different life problem. You won't hear the Giant thundering on those pages; they are not filled with *shoulds* and *oughts*. The law's voice is for the self-righteous and self-confident. I trust that you have already encountered the Giant and experienced some self-exposure, painful though it may be. Rather, in those pages you will hear the gentle voice of grace. You won't be told what you *should* do but rather what God *will* do by His grace, as you co-operate in faith. Two verses from different hymns say the same thing—the first penned by Isaac Watts, and the second by Charles Wesley:

> But there's a voice of princely grace
> Sounds from God's holy Word;
> Ho! Ye poor captive sinners, come,
> And trust upon the Lord.

> By grace we draw our every breath;
> By grace we live, and move, and are;
> By grace we 'scape the second death;
> By grace we now Thy grace declare.

CHAPTER 4

NEW COVENANT LIVING

At the very center of Christianity is a covenant-making God. All through history He has dealt with man through making covenants. A covenant is the initiative that God takes in establishing a solemn agreement, or promise, to redeem people and make them His own. There are two great covenants, the old one and the new one. The old covenant came through Moses on Mt. Sinai and the new one came through Jesus on Mt. Calvary.

There are many negatives connected with the old covenant. It was written on stone and its provisions were purely external. Its ministry was one of condemnation which led to death. Its glory was seen on only one man's face, and that was a fading glory. It was ratified or inaugurated merely by the blood sacrifice of animals, which had to be repeated over and over again. Its message was "Keep the law perfectly or you die!" The emotion it produced in men was fear, as they stood at the base of the mountain, terrified at the darkness, gloom, smoke, and flashes of light.

The Scriptures teach that the old covenant, or testament, was only temporary. The writer to the Hebrews goes so far as to say that it has now become "obsolete" (Hebrews 8:13). Yet in spite of this fact, the vast majority of mankind is still trying to live under its terms. It is a pitiful sight to see man, in his own strength apart from God, trying to live up to a set of requirements that he will never be able to meet. One does not have to become Jewish or even join a works-oriented church to fall under this philosophy. It's the religion of the man of the street; and sadly it's even the mind-set of most orthodox evangelicals—man trying to please God by living up to a list of rules.

But there is good news to declare. A new covenant has come into being to replace the old. It was announced at the Last Supper by its mediator the Lord Jesus Christ. Unlike Moses, this Mediator did not fall to sin but lived a perfect life. He is the Son of God Himself and therefore can initiate a perfect and lasting covenant. This permanent agreement with man offers eternal redemption, eternal life, and an eternal inheritance. These promises will never come to an end.

The message of the old was "Do this and do that. . . . Thou shalt and thou shalt not." It was a vocabulary of *shoulds* and *oughts*. But the message of the new agreement is one of promise. Its language is characterized by God affirming, "I will. . . ." He says to us, "I will forgive you . . . I will be your God . . . I will write My laws in your heart." It is no

longer an external rule book, that brings condemnation . . . but a heart change, that brings justification. There is no longer the fading glory on one
man's face, but the inner transformation of character in the hearts of all believers. The old covenant
prescribed requirements and standards that no
sinner could actually meet. But the new offers a
promise that any man with faith can receive. That's
good news!

How was such a new and wonderful covenant
brought into existence? With what was it ratified?
The answer to this question is the main theme of the
whole Bible. The new agreement was inaugurated
with a red liquid substance called blood. It was not
a great quantity, perhaps six or seven quarts, which
is the amount of blood in an average adult—certainly far less than the thousands and thousands of
gallons which were used in the animal sacrifices
under the old covenant. But this blood was special!
It was innocent blood, that which flowed in the
veins of a sinless man. It was Divine-human blood
in that it belonged to the Son of God. It was
precious blood in that it was able to pay the price of
the world's sin and redeem all who put their trust
in it.

This blood represents the scarlet thread that is
woven all through the fabric of the Old and New
Testaments. It's the primary message of the Bible—
that Jesus Christ has redeemed His people with His
blood. The great Prophet, Priest, and King has
made the perfect sacrifice that never has to be

repeated; and He has now been seated at the right hand of God, His work complete.

There is an old tale of three people who tried to gain entrance into heaven. The first was a rich man. He was asked by the angel for the password. He replied that he had contributed generously to his church, his morality was impeccable, and he was respected by all who knew him; therefore, he had earned heaven. But the angel said, "Wrong password." The second seeker was a distinguished man of the cloth. When asked for the password he answered that he had served the Lord for years, performed many righteous acts, and had been honored by many renowned institutions; therefore, he deserved heaven. But the angel said, "Wrong password!" The third person seeking entrance into heaven was an old woman whose body was bent with toil; but she had a twinkle in her eye. When asked for the password she lifted her arms and burst into song: "The blood, the blood, it's all my plea. Hallelujah! it cleanseth me." The gates of heaven swung open wide. These are the emotions produced by the new covenant of Christ's blood. It's not fear at the base of Mt. Sinai but joy and confidence on Mt. Calvary, at the foot of the cross. It's not the stern warning of a "Keep Out!" sign but the warm, personal invitation of "Come unto Me . . . !"

The greatest storm a man could possibly face in life is the terror and gloom of standing at the foot of Mt. Sinai and facing up to the law's demands. The choice of means for handling this life-threatening situation is simple: either the law or the gospel, the old covenant or the new, Moses or Jesus. It is a choice between man *trying* or grace *giving*. The gospel declares what God has done in Christ to save us from the fierceness of His wrath against sin. All who run to the cross will be saved.

Many have accepted Christ's offer and inherited the benefits of the new covenant. Many have experienced the new birth, having their sins cleansed by the blood and receiving Christ's righteousness. They even celebrate the Lord's Supper on a monthly basis, hearing the familiar words, "This cup which is poured out for you is the new covenant in My blood" (Luke 22:20). Yet their inner lives are frequently spent under the tyranny and condemnation of the old covenant. They listen in their minds to the accusations of Satan and feel in their emotions an imaginary distance from God. Forgetting that under the new covenant they have perfect standing with God and have been joined into union with Christ, they spend their days in misery and unrest. They are new covenant believers living under old covenant rejection! The only solution is to resist the accuser, go back to the Mediator, and heed the words of John: "They overcame him [Satan] because of the blood of the Lamb" (Revelation 12:11). A conscious, daily appropriation of the finished work of Christ is the only remedy for the accuser's fiery darts.

The old covenant not only fails people struggling with a guilty conscience; it also disappoints those struggling with temptation. Because it is merely an external standard, there is no power coming from within to live up to its requirements. You can compare the old covenant to a brand new car sitting in your driveway. But the car has no engine. The paint job is spotless and it looks beautiful. The brakes are fantastic and will stop the car on a dime. The steering is faultless and can direct you wherever you need to go. But there is no power to get the car moving! You toil and sweat as you push the car from behind and somehow a voice from within tells you this just isn't the way driving was meant to be. That's the trouble with the law. It's great at stopping and directing, but there's no power to move your life. The gospel puts the engine back in the car! The new covenant supplies the one thing lacking in the old: power. "Who also made us adequate as servants of a new covenant, not of the letter, but of the Spirit; for the letter kills, but the Spirit gives life" (2 Corinthians 3:6). So the key word is Spirit. We have been joined to another, united with the Spirit of God; the engine is back in the car. We can now rest in the confidence that God is able by His Spirit within us to live out the Christian life.

Let me ask you a question. Are you living under the old or the new covenant? I did not ask if you had accepted Christ, but rather if your lifestyle is more characteristic of the old covenant or the new. How can you tell? Let me suggest a list of questions to ask yourself:

- Do you make up rules to discipline yourself, which you then break?
- Do you criticize yourself harshly when you fall short of perfection?
- Do you feel close to God only when you're doing a lot of religious activities?
- Do you feel distant from God when your religious activities decrease?
- Do you feel frustrated at your lack of power to live a holy life?
- Do you entertain accusing thoughts in your mind which cause you to doubt if you really are a true Christian?
- Have joy and spontaneity somehow disappeared from your spiritual experience?

If you answer "yes" to a majority of these questions, it tells you that although you may be born of God, with your name recorded in heaven, your daily life is being lived out under the old covenant. You are living a performance-oriented, man-centered, works-directed lifestyle and not experiencing the glorious liberty of the sons of God!

What will life be like under the new covenant? You can face each day with the absolute certainty that you are fully accepted by God because of Christ's blood. You now rejoice in the reality that totally apart from your performance, Christ and you are united as one. When you experience accusing and doubt-producing thoughts you recognize them as from the devil, and run to Christ and His cross for assurance. You are increasingly experiencing the Spirit's power which enables you to live a holy life. When you make mistakes and fail, it doesn't throw you into despair—because you know God is able to work through weak, less-than-perfect people. Your closeness to God does not depend on how many meetings you go to per week but rather it's a reality that you frequently affirm by saying, "Thank You, Lord, that You're with me even in this ho-hum day. I acknowledge and claim Your presence even in these secular activities."

But the essence of new covenant living is found in the word which this book is all about: grace. The old covenant may have been built upon the foundation of law, but the new covenant lives through the heartbeat of grace. It is more than simply "unmerited favor" by which sinners are made fit for heaven. Grace is *God's goodness in action*. It is His kindness being poured into unworthy people. It is His free choice to give His Son freely to former rebels. Grace is Jesus offering His fullness to empty people, His riches to poor people, His purity to dirty people, and His power to weak people. Grace is Jesus living in and through sinners in such a way that they fall on their knees and cry out in every blessing: "It's all of grace, / It's all of grace. / All my life is from His grace!"

J. I. Packer has said that "there do not seem to be many in our churches who actually believe in grace."[1] That's an amazing statement from a respected evangelical theologian. Perhaps it points to the reason why there is so much criticism and rejection in churches. Perhaps that is why there are so many church burnouts, defeated pastors, and worn-out elders. Perhaps that is why so many Christians are wiped out by self-hatred.

We need to recover the essence of new covenant living, which is grace—Jesus living through undeserving sinners. People under grace will practice the new covenant lifestyle. They will have confidence in God's goodness in spite of their badness. They will accept others because God has accepted them. They will throw out the imaginary list they carry around by which they hope to be accepted by others and God. They will receive the free gifts that grace offers and live a life of praise and thanks. But most of all, deep down at a gut level, new covenant people will believe that the goodness and kindness of God is presently, right now, on the move in their lives in spite of all that they are. That is grace: God's goodness moving into action in unworthy sinners, enabling them to live life in a totally new sphere.

This is new covenant living! It may not always be religious; but it's always spiritual, in that it affirms things to be true that God says is true. It is a lifestyle based on the assumption that God always keeps His promises. If this new covenant is at the very center of Christianity and is the primary theme of the entire Scriptures, should it not hold the central place in our hearts? When it becomes central in our thinking, we experience a new spontaneity based on confidence that the law is in our hearts. New covenant is at the center of what it means to be truly Christian.

So the choice is before us. We can choose Moses and his condemnation or Jesus and His justification. If we walk with Moses, he will lay heavy precepts upon our shoulders. If we walk with Jesus, He will establish solid promises under our feet. Moses offers law that burdens, but Jesus gives free grace that lifts and liberates. The downward gravitational pull of the law is constantly with us. There will frequently be that voice of Moses speaking in our minds that we just don't measure up: "You can't possible be close to God and in union with Christ. Look how you fall short." If we listen to that voice, we will follow Moses back under tyranny of the old covenant with all its negatives. But if we reject that message of our emotions and listen instead to the promises of grace, Jesus Himself will lead us into new covenant living. Are you living under the obsolete covenant of Moses or under the new and eternal covenant established by Jesus Christ?

The point is *not* that we are free to disobey the laws of Moses. Far from it. Jesus said that anyone who breaks these laws will "be called least in the kingdom" (Matthew 5:19). The point *is*, which system are we living under, the old or the new covenant?

The writer to the Hebrews says that we as believers have *not* come to the mountain of the law but we *have* come to the mountain of the gospel of Jesus (Hebrews 12:18–24). It is there with Jesus that we must plant our feet and determine never to go back to the old mountain of fear. Take your stand with Jesus and His new covenant and learn the joy of all the "spirits of righteous men made perfect" (Hebrews 12:23) who will be gathered there with you. On that mountain and under that covenant you will not hear the law speaking to condemn you, but the blood speaking to defend you. Don't let yourself be pushed off. Don't be drawn away. Don't listen to another voice but that of Jesus.

CHAPTER 5

GRACE AND HABITUAL SIN
PART ONE

Deep within each Christian is a longing for holiness of life and Christlike character. Often we feel a stark inconsistency between the smiling "Sunday morning me" and the irritable "Monday morning me." The struggle is often related to secret battles in one's inner life which are consistently being lost. It could be losing your temper with the kids, or mentally judging and criticizing others, or yielding to some morally impure habit, or indulging in lustful fantasies. For some it's overuse of the TV, while for others it's repeated overuse of credit cards.

Many have made a habit of overeating to such an extent that thoughts of food dominate their lives. Failed attempts at control often produce depression and self-hatred. Others are in bondage to pornography. What begins as a search for pleasure and excitement yields guilt, misery, and dishonesty. For each person the specifics of the habitual behavior may be different, but the bondage is the same. Solomon describes it accurately when he says, "The ways of a man are before the eyes of the Lord, and He watches all his paths. His own iniquities will capture the wicked, and he will be held with the cords of his sin" (Proverbs 5:21–22). The word "paths" means wagon ruts made by repeated use. When a behavior pattern is endlessly repeated it creates a psychological rut, and then binds the person to that pattern.

In spite of increased Bible knowledge and growing maturity in other areas, the bondage continues unaffected. Eventually the frustration of Paul begins to surface: "For I am not practicing what I would like to do, but I am doing the very thing I hate" (Romans 7:15). Sooner or later the cry rises up: "Wretched man that I am! Who will set me free from the body of this death?" (Romans 7:24). If the question is not answered, despair can set in, leading one to give up on the whole Christian life.

The Apostle Paul said, "All things are lawful for me, but not all things are profitable. All things are lawful for me, but I will not be mastered by anything" (1 Corinthians 6:12). He was determined to let absolutely nothing, even legitimate things, become his slavemaster. The only one that is to rule over us is the Lord Jesus Christ!

In Hebrews 12 we are exhorted to run the race set before us, throwing off the sin which can "easily beset us." The idea behind the phrase "besetting sin" is that type of failure which easily encircles the

Christian runner, like a long, loose robe, tripping him up. Phillips translates it "the sin which dogs our feet." Many people have a peculiar weak area in which they are vulnerable. All through life they find it easy to give in repeatedly to this particular temptation.

To tell these people "just say no" is a totally inadequate solution. You might as well tell a fish to stop getting wet. Habit patterns can be so strong that they operate the same way physical addiction does in the realm of substance abuse. To break out of the pattern something more is needed than a mere ethical exhortation. Listen to the Psalmist's heart cry: "Turn to me and be gracious to me. . . . And do not let any iniquity have dominion over me" (Psalm 119:132–133). David longed for the grace that would not only forgive him but also deliver him. The bumper sticker "Christians aren't perfect, just forgiven" falls short of our desires. We long to be more than "just forgiven." We also want to be delivered from the dominion which habits exert over our lives.

Repeated sin can be not only addictive, it can lead to tremendous feelings of hypocrisy and doubt. "If I can't stop this pattern, then maybe I'm not a real Christian after all," goes the reasoning. These doubts are not easy to handle since they seem to be supported by certain passages of Scripture. The Apostle John tells us that "in Him [Jesus] there is no sin. No one who abides in Him sins. . . . No one who is born of God practices sin, because His seed abides in him; and he cannot sin, because he is born of God" (1 John 3:5–6,9). This scripture offers little comfort to a person wrestling with doubt. It seems to say that a test of someone's new-birth experience is whether or not he sins. The person with a besetting sin will either ignore this passage and pretend it's not in the Bible or become plagued by devastating doubt.

Because every word of Scripture is inspired, inerrant, and authoritative in our lives, we are not free to ignore John's words or even to soften them. But several things will help in understanding them:

1. These words in 1 John 3 were written to those who were indifferent to sin and were saying that it was no big deal. If they were spiritual and enlightened, so they thought, they could get away with it. John writes to tell them of the seriousness of sin and its incompatibility with the Christian life.

2. In chapter one he addresses a different error (that one could be perfect) and there he asserts that absolutely every human being, both saved and unsaved, sins. "If we say that we have no sin, we are deceiving ourselves, and the truth is not in us" (1 John 1:8). So we begin by understanding whom the statement was written to and why. And we also understand by interpreting scripture with scripture that John is not teaching the sinless perfection of believers.

3. The verb "sins" is in the present tense and in the Greek it implies habit, continuity, unbroken sequence. It is not an isolated act but rather a settled direction of character. In other words, the Spirit is telling us not that a Christian can't sin but

rather that upon his new birth there comes within his nature a strong antagonism to unrighteousness. The ruling principle of his new life is not indulging in sin but fighting it. As John Stott has said, "Sin and the child of God are incompatible. They may occasionally meet; they cannot live together in harmony."[1] Therefore, a true Christian will not be characterized by the type of habitual sin which is not resisted and grieved over.

In my own battle with temptation and sin, I have often grown discouraged. Upon occasion I have even entertained that doubt, "Maybe you're not a true Christian after all." But the very fact that I grieved over my sin and wanted desperately to overcome it was a proof that I and my sin were not living harmoniously together. I had declared war against it precisely because I *was* a Christian and God's nature was at work within me. These inner battles did not characterize the people John wrote about. They persisted and continued in their sin while experiencing no inner conflict. They weren't even trying to overcome. But the life of a truly born-again one will, as someone has said, be characterized by a "truceless antagonism to sin."

The very fact that you are reading this chapter with intense longing for answers is an indication that you probably are born of God, that you do know Christ and that His nature does abide in you. You are not living in harmony with your sin but have declared war against it. So the question is not

"Am I truly saved?" but rather, "How can I conquer sin?" It is Paul's question of Romans 7 that demands an answer: "Who will rescue me?"

But the way we try to conquer sin is very important. Sometimes our very intense desire for holiness can lead to a misguided reliance upon rules. Paul warns against a legalistic approach with these instructions: "These are matters which have, to be sure, the appearance of wisdom in self-made religion and self-abasement and severe treatment of the body, but are of no value against fleshly indulgence" (Colossians 2:23). Spurgeon understood this truth when he expressed his own warning: "I fear that some of my brethren and sisters try to grow in spiritual life by adopting methods which are not of faith. Some think they will set themselves rules of self-denial and extra devotion—these plans are lawful, but they are not in themselves effective, for vows may be observed mechanically, and rules obeyed formally, and yet the heart may be drifting yet further from the Lord. . . . I have found in my own spiritual life, that the more rules I lay down for myself, the more sins I commit."[2]

In the next chapter, we are going to follow the story of a man who learned that truth. It is the description of three roads he travels in an attempt to rid himself of habitual sin.

CHAPTER 6

GRACE AND HABITUAL SIN
PART TWO

Tom was a sharp young fella and many called him teachable and gifted. After he accepted Christ he grew quickly and developed a real zeal for the Lord. But after a few years he began to slow down noticeably and friends observed that he had somehow lost the joy of his salvation. The problem was an inward one, a secret failure which he had never learned to conquer. Gradually he realized that conversion had not really changed him in this area and that he was more of a slave to his sin than ever. Like a drug addict, he found himself ruled and driven by an enemy force within himself — outwardly successful but inwardly defeated. His feelings of hypocrisy were so great that this misery drove him to a desperate quest for personal holiness. It was a journey which would consume nearly half his life. He heard a message on the necessity of immediate confession. Why wait till bedtime or Sunday church to ask forgiveness? Once a person has sinned, the only appropriate and obedient thing to do is to confess it to God right away.

The first road he traveled down was that of the "cleansed life." Through the practice of immediate confession he would find deliverance from guilt and shame. The Scripture promised that confession would lead to cleansing. "If we confess our sins, He is faithful and righteous to forgive us our sins and to cleanse us from all unrighteousness" (1 John 1:9). This was a solid Bible promise. So he was careful thoroughly to confess every failure he experienced. At first it was difficult to believe that God was *that* good and faithful to His promises. Would God continue to forgive after his giving in to the same temptation for the third or fourth time in a row? The 300th time in a row? Yet this is what Scripture taught and he found great comfort in knowing that all his sins were washed away and buried in the deepest sea. But because he was unable to forsake his sin as well as confess it, the depression returned and the feelings of hypocrisy only increased. It seemed to him that his life had become an endless ride on a ferris wheel at the park. Down he went into failure, up he soared through confession—only to plunge down again in failure and rise again through confession. Down and up, down and up, the cycle repeated itself endlessly. Would they ever turn the ride off? Could he ever get out of this vicious cycle? As morally correct and appropriate and biblical as confession was, somehow it hadn't delivered him from his basic problem.

The next road he traveled was that of the "disciplined life." Man's will was the key to everything. We can choose what we want to be—and his choice was for holiness. He began to structure and discipline every detail of his life. Self-denial was the key that would unlock the door to the victorious life. He denied himself all kinds of legitimate good as well as anything that brought him near temptation. He prayed more, fasted more, memorized more, witnessed more, and attended every meeting he could go to. Perhaps he could so fill his life with religious activity that there would be no room left for the besetting sin. He became active in his church and served on several committees. He led Bible studies, went on witness campaigns, and served on the visitation committee. He prayed daily and earnestly for the holiness without which no one will see the Lord. He memorized scripture that related to his problem and then quoted it out loud when he was tempted by the devil. He developed accountability with a trusted prayer partner and asked for prayer. With great zeal he pursued the disciplined life; yet his inner failure continued. So he redoubled his efforts and made rules for himself which were far stricter than any followed by those in his circle of friends.

Yet, when he was alone with time on his hands, the old pattern would resurface. Like barnacles on a ship, the old ways clung to his life. All of his self-imposed regulations and discipline were helpful; yet they didn't take away his free will to choose. In spite of constant vigilance against any careless-ness, he still failed. There had to be more to the Christian life than the power of self-will. As good as discipline was, somehow it didn't deliver him. He was totally exhausted by the effort.

It was then that he heard a message on the "victorious Christian life." Here was the promise of complete victory. Of all the roads he had trav-eled, this third one offered the most hope. He read every book on sanctification he could get his hands on. Was it a crisis or a process? Could he thor-oughly die to his old self and be forever filled with the Spirit? Some of the books assured him that his sinful nature could be killed like an old dirty spider and he would be led into perfection. Testimonials gave promise that a crisis turning point would make him a new man and he would be delivered from the constant fluctuation between the flesh and the Spirit. Preachers urged upon him total commitment.

So after years of searching, he made the decision. One day at church, after a particularly stirring message, he went forward to kneel at the altar. There in total commitment he once and for all died to self. In full consecration he yielded himself to be filled with the Spirit. Later that night he wrote this all out in the form of a covenant which he carried in his wallet from that day forward. Desperately he clung to the feeling that accompanied the experience he had kneeling at the altar. As the days moved on, the feeling slipped through his fingers. Worse yet, the besetting sin surfaced again in his life, like an inner tube that can't be held under water too long. This time the despair was enormous. This last road seemed to play a cruel trick on him, leading right back to the "defeated Christian life." The covenant he had now broken was still in his wallet testifying against him. Now he was not only guilty of the besetting sin but also had broken a sacred vow that he made to God in the covenant. The end product of the third road was more condemnation.

Now he was disillusioned not only with himself but also with the whole "victorious life" teaching. Questions began to swim through his mind. Wasn't this teaching a promise of perfection in this life? Did its followers really believe they were perfect? Hadn't he observed "sanctified people" who, although testifying to a crisis experience, lived very unloving lives? Didn't this teaching vastly underestimate the subtle power of the old nature in every man? All of these questions shouted for answers, but none came. He had now tried the cleansed life, the disciplined life, and the victorious life—and failed miserably at all three. He began to feel that what worked for others did not work for him. He was different, weaker, more sinful, more willful. His faith was being shaken to its very foundation.

At this point of despair and confusion, he made

a very important decision, although at the time it seemed quite insignificant. He decided to put aside all his books, tapes, testimonial magazines and teachings he had heard, and just study the Bible. He was spiritually empty and emotionally broken, but he still believed there were answers to be found in the Bible. So he read and searched and studied the pages of Scripture afresh. Over a period of time he discovered one great truth which appeared to be the major thrust of the Scriptures: Christ! The whole book was about the second person of the Trinity. His person, work, and offices were clearly the one unifying theme that held the Old and New Testaments together.

Jesus Christ was described as the Creator, Sustainer, Redeemer, Sanctifier and Healer. He was seen as the great Prophet, Priest, and soon-coming King. The more he studied, especially the Gospel of John, the more one central doctrine surfaced as the essence of Christianity: God in Christ, Christ in you! He also began to recognize that the Christian life was not difficult, it was impossible! Only Christ could live it. The truth of "Christ in you" made it all possible. His strength, His purity, His wisdom, His love and His self-control are inside of each believer because Christ is in each believer. He saw that through no merit of his own the Mighty Savior indwelt his weak, frail body and personality.

The more he rejoiced in the riches that were his in Christ, the more his man-centered struggle for holiness faded into the background. He was particularly taken up by the idea that this was not an experience to be attained but a fact to be realized. He began to take God at His word and simply assume that Christ was literally living in and through his life. The knowledge that the Divine Son of God could actually speak, act, and even think through his weak personality was amazing. What a joy it was to be free enough from self to care about others and actually see Christ loving people through him. This was perhaps the greatest by-product of his new confidence. Without his even realizing it, the besetting sin had quietly slipped out of his life. The potential to fail was still there, but it was almost as if he didn't "need" his sin anymore. The chains had been broken and he was now free to let God work through him.

The more he focused on Christ, the more he was able to put the pieces of the puzzle together. The "cleansed life" was important and not to be rejected. One cannot rationalize or justify sin. It must be confessed so that there can be cleansing. There is sufficient grace available to cover many, many failings. "Where sin increased, grace abounded all the more" (Romans 5:20). The promise is true that "the blood of Jesus His Son cleanses us from *all* sin" (1 John 1:7). We do "overcome by the blood of the Lamb" (Revelation 12:11 *NIV*). He also saw the value of the "disciplined life." We are to fear God and hate sin, as the Scripture says: "The fear of the Lord is to hate evil" (Proverbs 8:13). We are to stay as far from temptation as possible, as Solomon told his young son: "Keep your way far from her, and do not go near the door of her house" (Proverbs 5:8). Those who live without discipline are simply making provision for their own failure. "Put on the Lord Jesus Christ, and make no provision for the flesh in regard to its lusts" (Romans 13:14). Learning appropriate Scripture passages that relate to our sin and then meditating upon them and obeying them is following Christ's example. Jesus said we are to "live by every word that proceeds from the mouth of God" (Matthew 4:4 NKJV). The Son of God conquered temptation by using the Scriptures.

But he now recognized that confession alone or discipline alone could not deliver him from the power of sin. They were simply building blocks in the life of holiness. Christ alone was the foundation stone and any building toward godliness must be done on that Rock. He also saw that "The Victorious Christian Life" concept had led him to search after a mere *experience*. This feeling-oriented "blessing" was measured in terms of how many days of "victory" could be sustained in a row. It was a setup for future failure. What he needed was not the system of the victorious life but the Victorious One Himself!

Reflecting back on the other roads he had traveled, he began to see his error. He had tried to be holy without the Holy One. He had sought victory without the Victorious One. But now he had exchanged the exhausting effort of self for resting in the Faithful One. He had exchanged external rules for relying upon the Indwelling Lord. All of what he had longed for was now discovered in Christ Himself. This Person would never slip away from him as had all the feelings and experiences of the past.

He still fell occasionally and the subtle pull of the old nature was ever present. Perfection would have to wait until another world. But now the Perfect One was living His life in and through a very imperfect person. Despair had turned into praise, joy, and confidence. He had found a solution to his problem. It was not a program, not a doctrine, not a set of principles; it was a Person— the resurrected, indwelling, victorious Lord.

But why did this approach or theology "work" while the confession, discipline, and victory approaches did not work? The answer is discovered by understanding the interrelationship of spiritual warfare and faith.

CHAPTER 7

GRACE AND HABITUAL SIN
PART THREE

We cannot understand the severity of the battle experienced by the man in the last chapter unless we know something of Satan. In Revelation 12, he is pictured as the devouring dragon and the deceiving serpent whose title and self-determined job description is "the accuser of the brethren." The devil is the most diligent of workers because he accuses believers "day and night" with a constant stream of put-downs targeted at their self-concept and ultimately at their faith.

In the strategy of tearing people down, the evil one often uses a ten-step program. We could call it the ten-step spiral into the pit of accusations. It is into this dark and slimy hole that the accuser seeks to plunge the followers of Christ. Because the enemy is deceitful and clever, he is able to disguise himself at each of the steps and cause the Christian to be totally unaware of any enemy activity. So as I describe the descent, there will be no mention of

Satan . . . but make no mistake, the accuser is active at every level.

1. A thought enters the mind. It is not good, but neither is it sin yet. This is simply temptation. All sin begins in the mind at this level.

2. The thought is entertained and acted upon. There is an inner yielding to that which is wrong. Indulgence turns the temptation into sin.

3. Feelings of guilt emerge. There is a new coldness in the spiritual life, a strange hardness in the heart; God seems further away, estranged, unapproachable. Shame becomes an inner reality.

4. "I am a hypocrite." The thought burns into your consciousness: "I live two lives." One life is known by your friends and the other known only to you. The whole downward spiral could have stopped just before this step but now a serious conclusion of self-identity has been made. This conclusion blocks any desire to pray.

5. Fixation on self. Suddenly the focus shifts from one specific failure to a whole generalized series of failures. The needs of others are totally out of the picture. Only one person is under scrutiny here and that is self.

6. The cross is forgotten. The name of Jesus is strangely absent from your lips and the blood of the new covenant foreign to your thoughts. The grace, mercy, and forgiveness of Christ are a thousand miles away. This step of the descent is so silent and invisible that one is rarely aware that he has forgotten Jesus Christ.

7. The towel is thrown in. You are no longer fighting against sin. If so many battles have been lost in the past, why try to resist any longer? A generalized hopelessness about the future emerges.

8. Irritability sets in. You are harsh and critical with

those closest to you even though they've done nothing wrong. You're upset with yourself but you take it out on others.

9. Depression takes over. This is not clinical depression requiring hospitalization, it's a low level sadness. The spark of life is gone. The twinkle of the eye has disappeared. A settled unhappiness is now accepted as the norm. Any Christian service is out of the question. After all, you are unworthy.

10. Vulnerability to further temptation. There is no strength or even reason to resist. The mind is now a fertile field for further evil seeds to be sown. The process can now easily start all over again with step one. "What damage could further sin do since there has already been so much failure?"

This is the pit of accusation. It is carefully constructed by the devil himself and personally administered by his cohorts against sincere Christians. If one is not serious about his Christianity, the enemy will leave him alone. But let a disciple get committed and he will suddenly find himself the target of spiritual attack. The devil doesn't care if Christians are rich or poor, healthy or sick, if only he can destroy their fellowship with God. That is the evil intent behind the whole ten-step spiral of accusations.

How does one get out of this pit of accusation? The answer is clearly given to us by John. "They overcame him because of the blood of the Lamb" (Revelation 12:11). In other words, it's going back to the finished work of Christ which He accomplished upon the cross for us. It is not looking forward to future victory but back to the historical sacrifice of the Lamb of God on Calvary. It is not confidence in our ability to overcome temptation or even in our sincerity of grief after we have fallen, but simple faith in the power of Christ's blood. It is confidence in grace rather than trust in works that allows us to climb out of the pit of accusation and overcome the devil and his hosts.

The nature of this warfare is not primarily a battle of the will against temptation. Rather it is a fight of faith to believe the promise regarding the blood of Christ. Paul describes it in his exhortation to stay in the battle and "fight the good fight of faith" (1 Timothy 6:12). Regardless of how true or false the enemy's accusations are, the question remains, will we accept by faith the payment of Christ's blood to make us clean? Do we believe the blood is powerful enough to make us acceptable to God? The apostle describes how we may appear before the searching eyes of God when we are trusting in the blood: "He has now reconciled you in His fleshly body through death, in order to present you before Him holy and blameless and beyond reproach— if indeed you continue in the faith" (Colossians 1:22–23). The phrase "beyond reproach" literally refers to a legal state of being free from accusation, unchargeable before the penetrating gaze of the judge.

Therefore, the center of the storm is points six and seven in the descent into the pit of accusations.

Are we going to listen to the accuser and quit fighting sin, or are we going to listen to the message of grace written in Christ's blood? To do the second is to pick up the shield of faith, get back on one's feet and resume the conflict against sin, confident that we are now clean and acceptable before God. In the 1988 Olympics in Seoul, a Korean fighter was distraught because of a decision against him. So, as a protest, he plopped down in the ring and simply sat there for over an hour. Now, as Christian warriors, we don't sit down in protest, but we often drop out of the battle due to discouragement with ourselves. There we sit, hour after hour, while there are many other battles that need to be fought. We have thrown in the towel, given up the fight, dropped out of the competition. The old saying is true: "A failure is not one who fails, but rather one who fails and then gives up."

To mix the metaphors—I have frequently fallen into the pit of accusations and then plopped down in the ring and given up the fight. But graciously, God has nudged me back into belief in the promises, and wearily and shamefacedly I've struggled back to my feet, picked up my shield, and resumed my fight of faith. The man in the previous chapter had such an initial struggle with sin precisely because he was listening to the accuser. His positive deliverance came as he began looking at Christ and believing His promises. His new victories seemed effortless, yet they represented a man learning to focus on his Captain and fight the good fight of faith.

To give in repeatedly to one sin can not only open us to the devil's accusations but also give him a "foothold" in our life (Ephesians 4:27). Therefore as deliverance takes place it is appropriate to take a stand of faith by renouncing the devil and all his ways and then submitting to Christ's lordship. Through this battle strategy that enemy stronghold is broken and we are free fully to exercise our faith in Christ and His victory on the cross.

To resist temptation and sin is only half of the battle. The other half is to maintain faith in our Leader. The writer to the Hebrews puts the negative and the positive exhortations together when he says, "Lay aside every . . . sin . . . , fixing our eyes on Jesus" (Hebrews 12:1–2). So the Christian runner is to run with his mind fixed on Christ. The Christian fighter is to stand with his faith grounded in Christ. And the accused brethren are to climb out of the pit with their confidence in the cross of Christ. "They overcame Him because of the blood of the Lamb" (Revelation 12:11).

CHAPTER 8

GRACE AND SELF-ESTEEM

If you were asked to describe yourself, what would you say? What kind of a "self-concept" do you carry around in your mind? The way we think of ourselves is absolutely vital to our spiritual health. It determines how we act, talk and feel, and can even have a great influence on our physical health. It affects how we view God, our friends and neighbors, and especially our family. People with a poor or unrealistic self-image have problems in every area of their lives. This image is something like the coach of a football team: he influences and shapes the overall personality of the team and many times calls every play. In the same way, the set of thoughts we have about who we are determines the outcome of our lives.

A child is told, "You'll never amount to anything!" He believes this and then spends the rest of his life fulfilling it. A young woman decides, "Nobody likes me." She then spends the next twenty years looking for examples that prove her right and denying examples that might disprove her theory. On the opposite side of the coin, an excessively overweight man who has just been fired from his job and divorced by his wife goes through a time of deep soul-searching. He concludes that he is loved by God and that he *does* have something to offer to the world. From that day forward his life begins an upward swing toward fulfillment, usefulness, and deep inner happiness. Our thoughts about ourselves are powerful and influential and demonstrate the principle that "as a man thinks in his heart, so is he."

Many people, even some Christians, think about themselves through the eyeglasses of the law. Because these eyeglasses are perfection-oriented, they focus upon and magnify all of one's failures. When such a person has a week in which everything goes well, then he feels good about himself. But if things are less than perfect, his self-esteem drops. In a fallen world, guess which state is more common! So these people become performance oriented in order to reach up toward perfection. It is a man-centered attempt to establish some way to feel good about yourself. Using these "law-eyeglasses" dooms a person to failure every time. Perfection is the standard, performance is the method, and depression is the outcome.

There is another way to attain a healthy self-esteem. It's called the gospel of Jesus Christ. Listen to the words of Paul, "But now apart from the Law the righteousness of God has been manifested . . . the righteousness of God through faith in Jesus Christ for all those who believe; for there is no distinction; for all have sinned and fall short of the glory of God, being justified as a gift by His grace through the redemption which is in Christ Jesus" (Romans 3:21–24). Because I have accepted and trusted in Christ's sacrifice on the cross, God now, through grace, sees me as righteous. It's a whole new pair of glasses to see myself through!

Here's how these "glasses" work. As I put them on, the reality that first impresses me is that I see all men are sinners. Everyone is falling short of the mark. Then I look at myself. All the mistakes, failures, and sins are still there but now, through the eyes of faith, I see that grace has made me *acceptable to God.* I take a second look just to make sure it's true. Yes, God in His perfection has accepted me totally apart from the law's demands and my performance. This is great! Now I don't have to perform to be accepted. Now I can accept *myself.* Now I can live with "me" and really get to like me. I have a whole new outlook upon myself.

There are orthodox, evangelical, born-again, Spirit-filled Christians who've been saved for years but are still wearing the old law-eyeglasses! How regrettable! Let me make a suggestion if you find *yourself* to be one of these frustrated, performance-oriented people. Are you uncomfortable? Go to the Doctor and get a new prescription. You will find your new glasses in Romans 3:24. Throw away the old glasses and start living a whole new life! See yourself by faith, the same way God sees you. It will begin to affect you in *new* and *wonderful* ways because, as you think in your heart, so are you.

The Apostle Paul was perhaps one of the greatest of all men and certainly one of the most influential. Yet, before his greatness could rise to the surface, there were some issues in his past that had to be dealt with. As a Jewish Pharisee, he had been the most zealous anti-Christian in the known world. He treated Christians with contempt, persecuted them, threw them in jail, and even oversaw the first execution of a Christian, the violent stoning of Stephen. As a new convert to Christianity, this past history could have haunted and destroyed any potential he had for serving Christ. But one concept penetrated his mind with blinding force and healing power. It was the concept of *grace and mercy*, and it proved to be the foundation of all that he taught and lived.

"I was formerly a blasphemer and a persecutor and a violent aggressor. And yet I was shown mercy, because I acted ignorantly in unbelief; and the grace of our Lord was more than abundant. . . . Christ Jesus came into the world to save sinners, among whom I am foremost of all" (1 Timothy 1:13–15). John Stott has commented that there was no way for Paul to have taken a scientific survey of all sinners who ever lived and then compared himself with them. When he said he was the "worst," it was a deep personal realization of the sinfulness of his sin. Once a man sees his own sin, it matters not how sinful someone else is.[1] Paul was able to deal with his past because he came to grips with the grace of God. He didn't ignore his past sins or deny his present sin nature. Instead, he believed and received grace which transformed his past failures into present testimony. Through grace he was able to *conquer* guilt and inferiority.

For each one of us there are things in our past that we are ashamed of—failures and sins which affect our concept of self and destroy our potential. I once worked as a teacher and track coach in an inner-city school. It was the tense time of the late 60's and the cities were like bombs ready to explode. After a particularly controversial and nervous track meet, my team ran for the school bus that would take us back to our school. Suddenly hundreds of kids appeared from nowhere and began stoning the bus! Every window in the bus was broken, and later that night my wife picked tiny pieces of glass from my scalp for about an hour. But the worst part was my instruction to the bus driver to "close the doors and drive away." Outside, two of our team members were left in the crowd and later were taken to the hospital. For days my mind was flooded with accusing thoughts. "You blew it. . . . You're a coward. . . . You saved yourself. . . . You left the kids to the crowds. . . ." It was only by acknowledging moral responsibility for my failure that I could live with myself. *Grace was available to cover my past with forgiveness and to provide for my future with hope.* At the end of that year, I was amazed when a Christian organization called me into full-time Christian service. It was only by the power of grace that I could forget what lay behind and press on toward the goal (Philippians 3:13). Past failures can either destroy us or be transformed into present testimony which exalts God's grace. Apart from this grace, I would have been destroyed by feelings of failure.

For some the problem with their self-concept is not past failures but present weaknesses. They reinforce these weaknesses by constantly speaking of them to others: "I have a poor memory. . . . I'm so disorganized. . . . I'm too sensitive. . . ." They don't realize that focusing on their weak areas produces fences which set boundaries for their usefulness. "I can't do this. . . . I'll never be able to. . . . You'll have to find someone else for that. . . ." God is not terribly concerned about our weaknesses! In fact, He deliberately allows them to continue so that they will be channels through which His grace will flow. "My grace is sufficient for you, for power is perfected in weakness" (2 Corinthians 12:9). *Sufficient grace overcomes limiting weaknesses.*

We could handle our weaknesses better if we had a more biblical view of the self. As someone has said, we are not called to become something great but to contain a great Someone. We are not shining examples of perfection, but weak containers of the Perfect One (2 Corinthians 4:7). Picture a great shortstop who has won the Golden Glove award for his excellent play on the baseball field. The glove is not really "golden." It's not the source of the greatness. We would be foolish to think that anyone could pick up that "magic glove" and perform like the Hall of Famer. No, the greatness is not in the glove itself but in the hand which it contains. We are like that old leather glove, weak and frail in ourselves. But when Christ enters our life, it's like a strong and skillful hand has just been inserted in the glove and now it's a "golden glove"— still weak and frail in itself, but doing great things because of who's inside it.

Our self-concept begins with being poor and weak. But it ends with the fantastic privilege of being containers of the Divine. Christians are the body that Christ walks in, the mouth He speaks with, and the hands He serves with. We are not simply weak earthen vessels but weak channels through which God's strong wisdom, power, and love flow to a needy world. Has this realization of being a container begun to affect and improve your image of yourself?

While many wrestle with past failures and present weaknesses, others are defeated in their view of self by *pride*. Again the remedy is grace. It is the weapon by which we will conquer pride. King Nebuchadnezzar had a serious problem with inflated thoughts of himself. He had been warned to acknowledge God as the Sovereign Ruler and source of his greatness. He ignored the warning. One evening he took a stroll on the terrace of his palace and saw the splendor of the city and empire he had built. Commenting to one of his associates, he said, "Take a look at all this. It was all my vision and idea. It was pulled off by my power, leadership, and ingenuity. And I deserve the glory for it!" Immediately the king was plunged into a serious "mid-life crisis" which lasted for seven years. He roamed in the field behind the palace eating wild grass as his body hair and nails grew. Pride had turned a prince into an animal. John Stott says, "There is something fundamentally 'obscene' about pride, something offensive to the Christian sense of what is decent, something calculated to disgust."[2] It's a subtle and ever-present enemy. Only when Nebuchadnezzar humbled himself, acknowledged that "Heaven rules" and praised God as the sovereign source of all greatness, was his sanity restored. Praise filled the house and pushed pride out the door!

The king had an unrealistic view of himself and his achievement. He failed to realize that all things are from God, through God, and to God. *He* is the underlying source, power, and end of all human achievement. Paul would say it as follows: "For through the grace given to me I say to every man among you not to think more highly of himself than he ought to think; but to think so as to have sound judgment, as God has allotted to each a measure of faith" (Romans 12:3).

It's not just heathen kings who have problems

with pride; Christians are also vulnerable. J. B. Phillips describes his experience with pride in his autobiography *The Price of Success*. After translating the New Testament, he was thrust into an immensely successful writing and broadcasting career. These were his words: "I was in a state of excitement throughout the whole of 1955. I was tasting the sweets of success to an almost unimaginable degree. My health was excellent; my future prospects were rosier than my wildest dreams could ever suggest; applause, honor and appreciation met me wherever I went. . . . I was not aware of the dangers of success. The subtle corrosion of character, the unconscious changing of values, and the secret monstrous growth of a vastly inflated idea of myself seeped slowly into me."[3]

But we need not be defeated by pride. Paul handled this enemy through the power of grace. It seemed that he was exalted as the greatest of the apostolic band. He won more converts, planted more churches, visited more areas, taught more sermons, and wrote more books than any of the others. Yet his self-view is pregnant with grace. Listen to his own description of how he saw himself and his accomplishment: "For I am the least of the apostles, who am not fit to be called an apostle, because I persecuted the church of God. But by the grace of God I am what I am, and His grace toward me did not prove vain; but I labored even more than all of them, yet not I, but the grace of God with me" (1 Corinthians 15:9–10).

The greatest of all apostles claimed to be the least! He did not exalt self but grace as the reason for his calling and success. He pictures grace as a motivating force that labors beside him and is responsible for all that he became and accomplished. Every successful person needs to follow this example and say of himself, "I am what I am by grace!"

So, let me ask you again the question we started with. What kind of self-concept do you carry around in your mind? For your past failures do you have God's grace to say to you, "They are forgiven and covered by the blood of My Son. You can live free from guilt and shame"? For your present weaknesses do you have God's grace to say to you, "Don't worry about them. You're just a container. Get your focus on the Divine Contents"? And for your achievements, do you have God's grace to say to you, "Be careful to praise Me. All that you are and all that you've done has been through Me; I'm the source of your success"?

One of the functions of God's grace is *to lift up the lowly and bring down the proud*. As James says it, the lowly should "take pride in his high position," and the exalted one is to "take pride in his low position" (James 1:9–10 *NIV*). The lowly man can say, "I have made many mistakes in the past and I have many weaknesses now, but I am a child of the King. I'm related to Royalty. I've been chosen to contain the greatest treasure on earth: the Lord Jesus Christ. He dwells within me and uses my personality to express His character to the world. I praise His grace!" And, in the same spirit of grace, the exalted brother can say, "In spite of all my successes, I know I'm simply a sinner saved by grace and no better than anyone else. All the accomplishments I've seen have been the direct result of God's work in my life, so He gets the glory. I praise His marvelous grace!"

Have you ever wondered what the purpose of all of human history is? Have you ever thought about the ultimate meaning and significance of your life and your personal history? It is clearly stated in Ephesians 2:7: "In order that in the ages to come He might show the surpassing riches of His grace in kindness toward us in Christ Jesus." The exceeding riches of His grace toward us will be the talk of the universe throughout all eternity! As trophies of His grace, we will shine with astounding glory. C. S. Lewis reminds us that there are no ordinary people in the universe. We are either immortal horrors or everlasting splendors. Receiving His grace causes us to shine in splendor. And God has determined throughout all eternity to show us off as examples of what His kindness can do in a yielded and trusting follower![4]

A portrait of a retiring seminary professor was unveiled. As the audience looked at it, the professor gave thanks and paid a well-deserved compliment to the artist. He said that in the future when people looked at the picture they would not ask, "Who is that man?" but rather, "Who painted that portrait?" The increasing glory with which *we* will shine will likewise point men to the *Master Artist*, the Lord Jesus. People will say of us, "Who *made* that man?" or "Who *made* that woman?" and we will answer, "Jesus Christ and the riches of His grace!" If this is going to be the topic of conversation throughout the ages, then perhaps we had better get on board *now* and begin to experience some of the exceeding riches of His grace.

CHAPTER 9

GRACE AND PHYSICAL ILLNESS

A mother sits next to the bed of her daughter in a hospital room. In the past two weeks, she has been told that her daughter has only one year to live, then that the x-rays were read incorrectly and she's okay, and finally that she is a very sick girl but it's treatable. Up and down go the emotions. Up and down goes the faith. It's a roller coaster from confusion to confidence and back to confusion again. In the long hours of the night the mother wonders where God is, and her daughter tries to determine what sin she is being punished for.

It is in the midst of pain and suffering that God's grace shines at its brightest. Perhaps one of the greatest insights into grace is revealed through the sickness a particular Jew experienced about 2,000 years ago. But before we look at that revelation, we must examine the broader teaching of Scripture on the subject of sickness and healing. We live in an age where many conflicting voices are heard on the subject: sickness is of the devil; God punishes through sickness; healing is in the atonement; it may not be God's will to heal; name it and claim it! What is a Christian to believe? What is the whole counsel of God on the subject?

The easiest question to begin with is, Does God have power to heal? The question is obviously and overwhelmingly answered in the affirmative by Matthew's Gospel. In chapters 8 and 9 there are ten great miracles of Christ grouped together. He shows His power over nature by stilling a storm, His power over the spirit realm by casting out demons, and His power in the moral realm by forgiving a man's sins. If this were not enough, He demonstrates His mastery over the various sicknesses which plague mankind. Each healing miracle seems to be representative of a category of diseases. First, He heals people with diseases affecting the whole body: leprosy, paralysis, fever. Then He touches people with local organic ailments: bleeding, blindness, dumbness. On a number of occasions we are told that He healed "all" and "every" sickness. "And Jesus went about all the cities and villages . . . healing every sickness and every disease among the people" (Matthew 9:35 KJV). The tenth and crowning miracle recorded by Matthew in this section is raising the dead! Is there anything too hard for God? The evidence drives us to conclude that there is no disease that God is not able to heal. All power belongs to Him.

The second question is a little more complicated.

Is sickness caused by sin? In finding the truth, balance is essential because there are at least two answers to this question. The first answer is, Yes, sickness could be caused by sin. Scriptures to support that are 1 Corinthians 11:30–31 and Psalm 32:3. If this is the case and the sufferer asks, God will always answer clearly. Can you imagine a father spanking his child, and when asked why, the father responds, "I'm not telling!" No loving father would do such a thing. The Lord's chastening is not punishment for a past deed but is correction to alter one's behavior in the future. Therefore, if God has sent some painful experience *as discipline* He is always willing to reveal the reason.

The second answer to the question is, No. Most of the time sickness is not caused by sin. Supporting scriptures for this assertion are found in John 9:1–3, where Jesus clearly states that a particular man's sickness was not caused by sin, and at Job 1:1, where God declares Job righteous and blameless and yet later he becomes sick. Let me ask you a question: Why are there weeds in your garden? Are they there because you sinned? If there is anyone to blame, it's Adam and Eve. There were no weeds before the fall of man. The first Adam was tempted in a perfect paradise; the second Adam, Jesus, was tempted in a wilderness. Something happened to the earth between those two men. It is recorded in Genesis 3:17–18. The physical universe was affected by the fall. Just as there are weeds in the ground, so there are germs in the air.

Most of the time we get sick simply because we live in a fallen world and we have caught one of those germs.

David Watson, the church-renewal teacher from Great Britain, saw many miracles of healing in his ministry. Yet he became ill with cancer himself and was forced to wrestle with this question. His observation is a clear description of the issue:

> Sometimes I have thought of my asthma or cancer as being a punishment for sins. . . . Is it conceivable that God should say, "Ah, there's David Watson. He slipped up rather badly last month so I'll afflict him with asthma for the next 20 years." Or later, "He's upset Me again, so this time I'll destroy him with cancer." Such thoughts are not only ridiculous, they are almost blasphemous—and utterly alien to a God of infinite love and mercy.[1]

The thing we need to avoid is becoming self-appointed spiritual doctors of people. There are courses offered to pastors, training them in how to determine the cause of someone's illness. There is biblical precedent for this, as seen in Paul's dealing with the Corinthian church; yet it can become a very dangerous thing when a whole group takes on this philosophy. A church can become very judgmental and eventually end up being "The Church of the Pointing Finger." Someone sneezes, and immediately there's a brother there judging the sin that caused the sneeze. Jesus said, "My *sheep* hear My voice," not "My sheep's *brother* hears. . . ." Job's friends took on this finger-pointing approach and God was not pleased with them.

God's plan for churches is that they be loving and accepting of people whether they are sick or healthy. We are to be "The Church of the Open Arms," that offers understanding and healing. Jesus is our model in this attitude, welcoming and receiving all who came to Him. Probably nine out of ten people in hospital beds are asking themselves the question, Why? It is not necessary that we know the answer to that question, but it *is* essential that we show God's love and acceptance.

The third question, like the first one, has an easy, obvious answer. What should we do when we are sick? The command of Scripture is to *pray for healing*, and as instructed in James 5, to request the elders of the church we attend to anoint us with oil. Oil is the symbol of the Holy Spirit, reminding us that it is God who does the healing. God's promise is that as the elders pray and anoint in the name of the Lord, the sick person will get well and be raised up. Recently I did a study in the Book of Acts, taking note of all supernatural events that occurred. There were over thirty references to miracles, and most of them were healings. You will also discover over thirty uses of the Lord's name there, such as in the healing of the crippled man: "Silver and gold I do not have, but what I have I give to you. In the name of Jesus Christ of Nazareth, walk" (Acts 3:6 *NIV*). This name was so powerful that the religious authorities commanded the Christians not to speak

or teach in the name of Jesus. Today, that name has
lost none of its power. He is the same yesterday,
today and forever!

Sometimes we are shy or hesitant to go before
God in prayer. We feel unqualified or unworthy to
approach the throne of the great King. "Maybe the
apostles boldly prayed in Jesus' name, but they
were apostles. I'm just me." And so our minds
travel down this road of fear . . . and at the very
time we need God the most, we stay away from
Him. Behind all of this fear and hesitation is the
realization of our sin. "If I come to God in prayer
asking Him to do some great miracle, won't He see
my great sin and reject my request?" It's kind of
like a schoolboy who can only be helped in his
request by one man, the principal. Yet that is the
one man he fears the most, because he knows the
principal is aware of some of his past misbehavior.

John Newton answered the dilemma simply in
his great hymn "Amazing Grace." "'Twas grace
that taught my heart to fear, / And grace my fears
relieved; / How precious did that grace appear/
The hour I first believed!" It was grace that first
taught us to respect, fear and honor God as we
learned of His holiness and complete separation
from sin. But it's also grace that relieves our fears
and bids us to come just as we are. The One whom
we fear the most is also the only One who can help
us; and under His wing is the safest place to be. To
paraphrase the writer of Hebrews: Jesus is a great,
high, and holy priest—but He has also been down

in the trenches with us. He has been tempted, and He knows what we're going through although He never gave in to temptation. Because His basic attitude toward us is not condemnation but *sympathy*, we should feel quite bold to approach His throne of grace in prayer. He won't disdain and reject us but will rather give us the grace that is needed to carry us through our difficult times (Hebrews 4:14–16)! We often expect God to be on an unapproachable judgment seat; but to our delight we discover He is enthroned on a mercy seat. And to that throne of grace He draws, invites, welcomes, urges, and even commands us to come!

It should be noted that the Bible is not against the use of doctors and medicine. Jesus spoke commendably of physicians (Mark 2:17), and Paul makes mention of "Luke, the beloved physician" (Colossians 4:14). Paul also encouraged Timothy to use wine as a medicine. Sometimes God will heal through prayer and sometimes through medicine. Both are the hand of God. In the case of medicine, God is wearing the glove of nature. In the case of prayer, He removes the glove and reaches down with His naked hand of power to touch a person, and we call it a miracle. In either case, *God* is the healer. He has provided prayer, elders, and people with gifts of healing and faith. He has also provided doctors, hospitals, and medicine. We have seen wonderful advances in medical science. I believe we also need to see an invasion of the supernatural in our midst. But both are to be welcomed as coming from God.

The final question we want to examine is, What are we to think when someone is not healed? Not long ago in our church two women came down with lung cancer within a few weeks of each other. We prayed and fasted. We anointed with oil. We looked to God for healing. The first woman received medical treatment but continued to decline. She became progressively weaker in spite of all our prayers. Eventually she died and our whole fellowship grieved her loss. The second woman was also in and out of the hospital; her doctors gave her three months to a year to live. But God touched her body. She was beautifully and miraculously healed; now, years later, only a scar remains in her lung, as a testimony to God's power. Medicine could not help her—but God could! Our whole fellowship rejoiced over this wonderful miracle. But why should one person be healed while another is not? Both were Christians and they had equally strong faith. There are mysteries that we simply do not understand! Moses tells us that the things revealed belong to us but the secret things belong to God alone (Deuteronomy 29:29).

We should never forget that everyone eventually dies, and ordinarily they go home to heaven through sickness. I believe with all my heart in divine healing, but I also believe God is sovereign and free to call a person home when his days are over. God is sovereign in His power to heal and we are correct and acting in obedience when we pray for healing. God is also sovereign in calling people home and we must submit to His Lordship in that too. Paul taught that to live physically was to know and experience Christ by faith, but to die was to gain a face-to-face relationship with Him. And that is far better than staying in this dark world! David Watson said that death is simply turning out the lamp at the dawning of a new day. Who needs artificial lighting when the bright sun is shining?

But what of the person who does not go home to be with the Lord, yet neither is he healed, but lingers in life, suffering through sickness and pain? Today we are hearing counsel given which just doesn't fit the Scripture. It goes something like this: "Satan wants you sick, but God wants you well. Healing is provided for in the cross—so no Christian need be sick. Simply claim, in fact *demand* your healing, and it's yours! If you don't receive healing, it shows that you just don't have faith."

How are we to react to such assertions? There is some very faulty theology in the above statements. Yet the people who believe this often see more healings than those of us with more "correct" theology! But it's not shallow theology which God is honoring, but greater and simpler faith. They just believe God! This reminds us not to put God in a box, nor assume that we have the final answer on theology. *God will honor faith wherever He finds it.*

I do believe that in the cross of Christ provision is made not only for our spiritual life but also for our physical bodies. Matthew 8:16–17 makes reference to this. It could be said that all blessings, whatever their nature, flow in one way or another from the sacrifice of Christ on Calvary. But it does not follow that it's always God's will to heal. God often has higher purposes than to heal. He can use evil and suffering to benefit us. Job, who longed to be healed, came to a place of seeing God's higher purposes in his suffering and seemed to conclude that his healing no longer mattered (Job 42:2,10). It was at that point that God healed him.

Generally speaking, Christian prayer is not to be characterized by a demanding spirit but rather by the confident yet submissive spirit of a child approaching his loving father. Even so, there is a definite place in our prayer life for boldness and authority. This is particularly true in dealing authoritatively with the devil as Jesus did when He "drove out the spirits with a word and healed all the sick" (Matthew 8:16 NIV). We need to conform our prayers to the example of Jesus in this regard.

Probably the most misleading part of the assertion that it is always God's will to heal is that "when there is no healing, it shows there must not be enough faith." Very often our faith, as well as our body, is weakened by the sickness. We don't have the strength to believe or even to pray for ourselves when we are sick. That is where fellow-believers come in. When the paralytic was lowered through the roof, it says that Jesus saw their faith (that of the sick man's friends) and he healed the paralytic. But to accuse a sick person of not having enough faith is simply cruel. It springs from the arrogance of health. It's easy to say that to someone else when all is going well with yourself. And I would venture to say that there are probably no *perfectly* healthy people; talk to a man long enough and you will discover that even in his "health" he may have a sore back, or a bad knee, or headaches, or something else wrong. Just about everyone suffers from some unhealed problem. We *all* need God's grace to deal with suffering. And it's at this point that grace *shines* with its greatest brilliance!

The great Apostle Paul himself became sick. He tells the Galatians that this illness was the reason for his stopping in their city to preach the gospel (Galatians 4:13). He also tells the Corinthians in more detail about his bodily ailment. On three occasions Paul asked God to remove this "thorn" as he calls it. But God allowed the weakness to continue and gave Paul this reason: "My grace is sufficient for you, for [My] power is perfected in weakness" (2 Corinthians 12:9). Here we see human suffering and weakness deliberately allowed to remain in order to be a channel through which divine power can flow. Some will argue strongly that this "thorn" was not a physical sickness. The fact is no one can say dogmatically what Paul's problem was. Volumes have been written on the subject. Most interpretations can be grouped into three possibilities: bodily pain and sickness, mental anguish in temptations, and human enemies and opponents. But the Spirit of God saw fit to leave the precise description of the "thorn" out of the Bible. No one knows exactly what it was. Perhaps it wasn't physical illness. But the vagueness which exists allows all with weakness to identify and apply it to themselves.

All we know is that it was something he strongly reacted against and wanted out of his life. This great man of faith prayed repeatedly for its removal. His experience gives us a principle as to how to handle similar frustrations in our lives, whatever they be. This unchanged condition was also used by God to keep Paul's pride in check and cause him to maintain a humble walk with the Lord. *The Amplified Bible* says it well: "My grace— My favor and loving-kindness and mercy—are enough for you [that is, sufficient against any danger and to enable you to bear the trouble manfully]; for *My* strength *and* power are made perfect—fulfilled and completed *and show themselves most effective —* in [your] weakness."

This verse is one of the mountain peaks of revelation in Scripture about grace. It is interesting that the context of this great teaching on grace is pain and suffering, pleading and frustration. These afflictions are the foothills out of which the mountain peak of grace emerges. Rarely do we experience grace arising out of placid pools of refreshing water or beautiful plains and meadows. It is in times of suffering that we feel our need for God most keenly.

Paul had many gifts and experiences which

would cause him to feel quite secure and sufficient. Receiving revelations from the third heaven would certainly qualify as a sufficiency-producing experience. But it's when we *don't feel sufficient* that we are open to see grace in all of its brilliance. When things don't go well at work, when people misunderstand and oppose us, when family conflicts intensify, when failure is repeated, when suffering is not removed—it's at these points of weakness that we realize how insufficient we are. The "thorn" Paul experienced was a messenger of Satan; yet at the same time it was God's chosen instrument to reveal grace. Regarding the interplay of the enemy and God, Joseph's words to his "enemy" brothers is pertinent: "You meant evil against me, but God meant it for good" (Genesis 50:20). Only God could take the destructive devices of the enemy and turn them into His positive blessings. Satan may have his design in our pain, but God's plan is higher and stronger.

At our point of need we cry out to God, "I'm not sufficient for this." We feel our need is for healing of our bodies or deliverance from our enemies or the smoothing out of conflicts or the granting of unbroken success. "*Then*," we think, "I will be sufficient." But sometimes God doesn't send those blessings. Instead He sends a greater blessing, His grace. And He says to us, "My grace is enough. It's all you really need. In fact, it's better than healing or deliverance or prosperity. Grace and spiritual power work best in weakness. *You may not be* sufficient but My powerful grace *is!*" This grace is the motivating force to get out of bed each day in spite of hardships we will face. His mercy is new and fresh each morning!

From all that we have seen, we can say without reservation that God has power to heal. When we are sick, we should pray in faith and in the name of Jesus that God will raise us up. We should pray boldly and confidently without doubting or giving God any escape clauses. We should claim the promises by faith and expect God to honor them. We should believe without reservation that He works through the prayers of the church elders and that healing is one of the church gifts (1 Corinthians 12:9). In this day of confidence in science and skepticism toward God, we need to affirm increasingly our faith in a supernatural God who can break through into the natural realm.

But if we are not healed we should not despair, because we can find grace not only to cope but also to prosper and abound. In fact, as we acknowledge our weakness a strange yet wonderful phenomenon occurs. God builds a tent over our heads! Paul concluded, "Therefore I will boast all the more gladly about my weaknesses, so that Christ's power may rest on me" (2 Corinthians 12:9 *NIV*). The word "rest" means to tabernacle or pitch a tent. The tent is filled with power, and it goes wherever we go so long as we acknowledge our weakness. Many men of God can testify along with Paul to extra power being released in their ministry when they were at their weakest. So there is both grace to heal and grace to cope and prosper in affliction.

I have two friends who exemplify this truth in quite an amazing way. One has muscular dystrophy and is basically confined to bed with only occasional trips out in her wheel chair. Yet she has managed to teach, first a junior high boys' Sunday School class and now adult classes. She is actually one of the best Sunday School teachers I've ever known. The power of Christ is flowing through her limp body. My other friend has multiple sclerosis and has had to take early retirement and spends at least half his days resting. Yet he manages to lead a weekly Bible study, teach a weekly discipleship class at church, and shares his testimony frequently at various meetings around the state. God's power has pitched a tent over both of these people and He is using them in amazing ways! There is grace that is sufficient for *every need!*

We may not understand the *why* behind our suffering; but God's grace is able to show us that there is a divine design behind all of our troubles, giving them purpose and meaning. Listen to how the hymn writer expresses it: "When through fiery trials thy pathway shall lie,/ My grace, all sufficient, shall be thy supply;/ The flame shall not hurt thee—I only design/ Thy dross to consume and thy gold to refine." Suffering is frequently the best method to burn away the dross of our self-life and bring to the surface the gold of Christ's life within us.

There is probably nothing in life that causes a person to search his heart more than illness. Pain and suffering are very effective in bringing us to our lowest points. But at the same time, grace can transform the most difficult experience into the greatest source of character growth, increasing one's maturity and deepening his peace. We always learn more through times of tribulation than in times of tranquility. I have spoken to countless people in hospital beds who testified to the increased activity of God in their lives and to their own increased teachableness.

So what is our conclusion as we look at human suffering and pain? God is *able and willing* to shower undeserved grace and blessing upon each one of us! We may find it at the throne of grace in answer to simple prayers. We may receive it through gifts of healing given to people in the church. We may experience it through new power which is magnified in our weaknesses. Whichever way, God's undeserved goodness and strength is all that we need! His *grace* is sufficient.

CHAPTER 10

GRACE AND TRUTHFUL SPEECH

More damage has been done by the human tongue than was ever inflicted by bullets or bombs. Deeper wounds have been received from words than ever from sword or spear. Unlike torn flesh, the spirit heals very slowly from word-wounds. Accusation, condemnation, rejection, judgment and curses have all issued forth from men's mouths. Careers have been hindered, reputations sabotaged, schools disrupted, churches split, friends separated, business distracted, ministries weakened, confidence shattered, and hope destroyed—all by the power of the tongue.

James tells us that although the tongue is a small part of the body, it has unusual power and influence. It is like a tiny spark jumping from a smoldering camper's fire in the woods. Although less than an eighth of an inch long, that tiny spark can blacken and kill eighty-foot-high trees and wipe out and destroy hundreds of acres of forest. Once the spark has begun its devastating work, thousands of people will have to labor day and night just to control the spread of destruction—but never can undo its damage. So it is with the human tongue. One little sentence from our mouth can start something that may grow into a totally unmanageable holocaust!

Words also have great constructive, upbuilding power. The universe was created through God's words and He presently sustains it through His word of power. In personal relationships a word can encourage, uplift, sustain, strengthen, or comfort. A word in season comes at the precise moment of need and says exactly what is required to help a person overcome or go on in his walk of faith. Solomon says that conversation from a righteous man's lips can be compared to a beautiful and refreshing fountain of cool water. It produces life wherever it flows. So, under the control of the Spirit of God, the tongue can do a great amount of good.

How can we make our words more like the fountain of life and less like the destructive forest fire? How can we use our words to heal rather than wound? How can our tongue become a source of creation rather than destruction? The answer is found in looking to Jesus Christ as our model. He demonstrated a perfect balance that no other human being has attained. He was full of grace and truth simultaneously.

John tells us in the first chapter of his Gospel that "the Word became flesh" and we observed His life.

What men saw when they looked at Jesus was that He was filled with graciousness and truthfulness. Now we have all known people who are strong in grace but weak in truthfulness. People of this sort have a strong urge to be accepted by others and will often sacrifice their integrity to make people continue liking them. For instance, someone asks them what they think of some particular musical performance. Deep down they really disliked it, but they submerge their true feelings and answer with a polite statement of how good it was. This is grace without truth. It's a form of graciousness which is really *not* grace, but simply shallow niceness which seeks to be accepted by everyone. It is weakness that springs from insecurity and fear of rejection, and often leads to insincerity, flattery, and even dishonesty.

Grace without truth creates a blob personality. People of this kind don't ring true. You begin to detect that they are not expressing their true feelings but are just being nice. They have mistaken niceness for graciousness and lost the courage and spontaneity that allows a person to be himself. On the other hand, true grace is not being obnoxious but rather means being sensitive to others' feelings and avoiding unnecessarily hurting others. True grace allows one to say, "This is how I see it . . ." or "My inclination is. . . ." It expresses true feelings without harshness or rejection of others. When Jesus spoke, people were impressed with the graciousness of His words, yet they knew He would never compromise just to fit in. Is it okay to be dishonest or deceive someone because we don't want to hurt his feelings? The answer is No, it is not okay. Although we don't need to tell people absolutely everything, what we do say needs to be the truth; and we are not free as Christians to create false impressions. That is simply another form of dishonesty.

Others have the opposite problem. They are truthful to a fault. No one fails to learn what their mind is on the subject. They speak the truth as they see it, but not in love. They say the right thing in the wrong way. The great car maker Henry Ford was a genius of a man. With his assembly line and the Model T, he brought the automobile to the common man. He became a multi-millionaire and his influence upon the nation, and even the world, was immense. But he treated his only son, Edsel, with harshness and disdain. He crushed him with rejection and often embarrassed him publicly with cutting words. Some feel that Henry Ford drove his son to an early death. Greatness and graciousness are often seen as opposites in this twisted world.

Christians need to speak the truth—but not in a way that slashes and wounds. There is a proper way to tell the cold, hard facts. A shoe salesman bluntly told a woman, "Your foot is too big for this shoe!" His colleague had a different approach. He would say with kindness, "Ma'am, this shoe is too small for your foot." It doesn't take great skill to be gracious, just a little sensitivity. Paul tells us in

Colossians 4 that our conversation with outsiders needs to be full of grace and tastefully seasoned with salt. Too much witnessing is done in a way that offends and turns people off. In contrast to this, we need to heed Paul's words and learn how to fill our words with grace. Someone has said that a graceless witness is a blind man elected to a professorship of optics, philosophizing on light and vision— while himself being absolutely in the dark. Without grace a witness is a mole professing to educate eaglets. If we are saved by the grace of Christ, then we need to show some of that grace as we talk with the lost about this God of grace!

Jesus alone stands out as the one who perfectly balances the gentleness of grace and the strength of truth. He was able to maintain the courage of truthfulness while not sacrificing the beauty of grace. He boldly confronted the leaders of His day, fearlessly speaking the truth. But in His personal conversations we see the beautiful balance of truth and grace. He went right to the sore spot with the rich young ruler, counseling him to dethrone money in his life; yet His confrontation was tempered with deep love. With the woman at the well He also moved in on the most sensitive issue of her life: the five divorces and remarriages she had had, followed by living immorally with a man. Yet He spoke this truth in such a loving and sensitive way that the woman actually went back to town and brought all the people out to meet this man! The downtrodden and rejected always felt comfortable in His presence. The "bruised reed"–type people He never broke and "the dimly burning wick"– type people He always fanned into flame. After a speaking engagement in His home town, everyone, Luke tells us, spoke well of Him and the people were amazed at the gracious words that came from His lips.

What modifications can we make in our speech in order to become more gracious? The first step is to *begin thinking toward others with the same mercy and understanding with which we think of ourselves.* Most people are forgiving toward themselves but judgmental toward others. Keith and Gladys Hunt point out the self-deception we are often prone to:

I am firm; he is pig-headed and obstinate.
I share news; he carries tales and gossips.
I make a story interesting; he exaggerates and lies.
I have reconsidered; he has gone back on his word.
My child is independent; his child is a willful, spoiled brat.[1]

This kind of double standard never fosters grace.

The second change we can make to become more gracious is to *give the other person the benefit of the doubt* in times of conflict. "Perhaps you didn't mean this, but. . . . I'm sure you didn't intend to hurt me, but. . . . I don't expect this is true, but could you explain. . . ." Asking questions is always a better way of beginning a conversation than making accusations.

A third way to become more gracious in speech

is to *treat enemies with fairness.* People we don't get along with do have strengths. Human nature will often blind us to those virtues and lead to tunnel vision, focusing only on their weak areas. The gracious person does not pretend there are no weaknesses, but he does acknowledge the virtues of his enemies. In this way he is able to "bless and not curse" with his words.

These three practices can add grace to truth. They can give to us greater balance and caution in the way we speak. But without faith in the indwelling Christ, they are simply human techniques that go no deeper than the surface. How did Christ maintain such a perfect balance between grace and truth? His secret was faith in the Father who indwelt Him. In the Gospel of John, He asserts that the words He spoke were not His own; they came from His Father. God the Father gave Jesus not only what to say but how to say it. So the secret of the Son was to let the Father speak through Him. And the secret of the Christian is to let Christ speak through *him.* God in Christ, Christ in you. That's Christianity!

But we live in a fallen world and have sinful natures. We do fail to be truthful and fall short of graciousness. At those moments we have only two choices: defend ourselves, or acknowledge our wrong and get back on the right track. There is grace which is greater than all our sin . . . and we need not take the course of self-defense.

In some Christian circles it is thought to be

acceptable to engage in lots of critical talk about fellow believers. In fact, some consider it their spiritual duty to make critical judgments of others. It's almost as if they have developed a whole ministry around the "gift of criticism." Every opportunity is taken to cut down other Christians. They would never dream of committing one of the sins of the flesh (drugs or immorality) but don't think twice about falling into the sins of the spirit (gossip, judgmental attitude, critical/condemning spirit, or harsh and cutting words). It would even seem that some enjoy this activity as a recreational pastime! They wouldn't know how to spend their time without it. "After all, what else is there to talk about?" they reason. To backslide into such ungracious conversation is nothing less than murdering people with words. It is sin, that God will judge.

Isaiah the prophet had an encounter with God that shook him to the core of his being. He saw the terrible holiness of God and was instantly struck with the guilt of his own sin. He confessed to being a man of unclean lips living among a whole generation of people with unclean lips. The sins of the tongue had affected absolutely everyone he knew. God saw his repentant spirit and touched his mouth and cleansed his lips. From that day forward, Isaiah went on to use his tongue for God and became a great spokesman and mouthpiece for the Lord. We need such conviction and cleansing in our generation.

When our lips have been cleansed by the blood

of Christ and our tongues are controlled by the Spirit of Christ, gracious speech will result. Sometimes a soft answer is needed to turn away wrath. At another time it's a compliment where praise is due but not expected. There are some occasions when total silence is required—as was the case with Jesus not opening His mouth during His trial. But whatever is called for, God's grace is available to guard our lips and influence what is said. When we die to our sinful nature, then Christ is free to be expressed through our personality, which includes our speech. He is able to put His words in our mouths in a totally natural way that fits our uniqueness. What a fantastic God!

As we yield to Christ in this way, we will discover ourselves fulfilling Paul's words in Ephesians 4. Here is a loose paraphrase of what he says. "Don't let any rotten or unwholesome words flow out of your mouth and tear people down. Rather, speak words that build people up and affirm them. You can speak either judgmentally or redemptively. Choose that which is in the flow of God's purposes to save and edify people. If your words are carefully chosen and appropriately fit the need of the situation, you will see the grace of God being ministered to your listeners through your kind and tender-hearted ways."

This week I visited a Christian farm that rehabilitates drug addicts from the inner city. There were 350 men at the meeting, all in the process of being saved from their sin. As the meeting started, the leader called out six names and had these men stand. He then commended them simply but sincerely for having a good attitude that week in the machine shop. The biggest smiles you could imagine broke over these guys' faces and you could see their self-esteem rise as their friends applauded and patted them on the back. It was a beautiful example of a Christian leader using his words to affirm and build people up. We can and should express our love and care for people by the words of our mouth.

C. S. Lewis wrote about relationships, that we are to "take each other seriously — no flippancy, no superiority, no presumption."[2] This high view of others as God's unique creation stimulates even more love and carefulness in our speech. As we talk to and about other people, our words will increasingly be conformed to the character of Christ. As we take people seriously, we'll avoid mere shallow niceness (grace without truth) and will also avoid harsh bluntness (truth without grace). We will increasingly move toward the ideal Christlike balance. And as it was with Jesus, so it will be with us—that people will be amazed at the gracious words that come from our lips.

CHAPTER 11

GRACE AND SPIRITUAL MINISTRY

Life was meant to be an adventure. Effectively serving God and people does something to an otherwise boring existence. Someone once told me that life was like a bottle of pop and evangelism was the fizz in the pop. I believe that. There is something about personal ministry which adds excitement, joy, and meaning to life. It puts zest and adventure into your daily routine. To be the personal agents of a great King gives us a sense of importance. Having a ministry, however small, allows us to feel that we have some part in building God's kingdom on earth.

But many times we think it's impossible for us to be involved in some effective spiritual service. We say, "I can be an usher or have some other job in the church, but I'm really not qualified or gifted enough to touch others' lives." Along with this feeling of inadequacy comes a fear that God might ask me to do something I find totally disagreeable. He might make me preach on a street corner, and I'm terribly shy and hate public speaking. Or He might send me to Africa, and I really dislike moving and can't stand snakes. Behind this thinking lies the concept of a God (he's not the God of the Bible) who lives to make you miserable. This deity peers over the balcony of heaven searching for ways to cause people to cower and sweat. "You say you don't like kids? Good, I'll make you a school teacher! . . . You say you don't like water! Great, I'll make you a deep-sea diver! Ha Ha Ha Ha Ha!" No, this is not the God of the Bible. God is the creator of our personalities as well as our bodies. He made the peculiar features which make you distinctively you. He gave you the tendencies and leanings which have led you in certain directions. He is even responsible for giving you the set of parents you have. The Psalmist says that we were "woven together" by God in our mother's womb.

Legalism's approach to ministry is often disturbingly negative. "Don't ever say 'I never want to be a——' because that's exactly what God will make you do!" we are told. But what kind of a God goes about forcing people to do what they hate? We are often given the impression that to serve God involves doing things against our personality and offensive to others. Rebecca Pippert points out that many people feel they must offend in order to be a good evangelist, so they avoid ministry altogether. But our real problem, she says, is that we don't know how to be ourselves.[1] God, through His grace, is quite able to put His desires within us and merge them with our personality. The legalist is out there doing his duty because someone put him on a Christian-service guilt trip. But those under grace are blissfully going about *being themselves,* and in a wonderfully natural way God is using them.

So, perhaps the service God might want you to do is exactly what you would want to do! Perhaps the desires you have were secretly planted there by an all-wise Creator who wants you to stop imitating others and just be yourself! This does not mean that there is no self-denial or sacrifice or suffering in the Christian life. Denying our selfish ways is the starting point for knowing the resurrected Christ. The cross has always come before the resurrection and it always will. But is it not possible that the resurrected Christ, once He is unleashed in our lives, will live and express Himself through our unique personalities?

For some this is too dangerous a teaching. They envision weird people running around shouting, "I gotta be me!" and overlaying their egocentric ways with a spiritual veneer. They fear the fanatic who makes blanket statements claiming that whatever he does is what Christ wills. As careful people who have a healthy fear of the Lord, we realize that there are dangers, and that every doctrine can be twisted. But we don't throw out the baby with the bathwater. We reject the dirty bathwater (flesh doing its own thing), while holding on to the baby (Christ expressing Himself through us).

I used to think that a week of prayer had to

precede every decision I made. Praying for guidance is a valid part of the Christian life. But I had made prayer into a form of procrastination, and lots of opportunities for serving slipped by me. When Jesus saw a need He didn't run off to a prayer meeting. He just met the need! I have since come to realize the glorious freedom there is in spontaneously doing what I feel should be done and acting on the assumption that Christ was doing it in me! A. W. Tozer has commented that "once we see this truth there won't be a secular stone in the pavement." Cleaning the garage is just as spiritual as leading a Bible study; going on a picnic, just as valid as going to church. Jesus may want to shovel snow through me at one point, fast and pray through me at another point, and go jogging through me at another time. He may want to "borrow my body" to witness His love to a neighbor, and later that day go to a nice restaurant through me. If there is "no division between the secular and the sacred," and if we are united with Christ, then why do we try to lock Jesus into the church building, excluding Him from any activity that's not "religious"?

God has a work for you to do and it will definitely be the "fizz" of your life. But the way to discover it is not by denying the desires you have but by analyzing them carefully and then letting God fulfill them in your present circumstances. We tend to think of "God's will" or "finding a ministry" as something out there in the future, dangling before us but just out of reach. This causes us to live in a constant state of frustrated hope that is never fulfilling. In contrast to this, we can embrace the idea that *right now, today, in my present circumstances,* Christ wants to live His life through me. Faith then is not "believing something about a future day," but "acting on what I know to be true in the present." If I'm a true Christian, then the fact is that *Christ lives in me.* Faith is my acting on that truth and letting Him prove the fact.

A man grew increasingly frustrated with his insurance business. Deep down he had a desire to do counseling. He also had a passion for evangelism and an ability to relate well to those we might call "hard cases." A friend asked him to visit her son in prison, and he immediately followed through on this opportunity to serve. One contact led to another, and soon he was visiting fourteen or fifteen men. This led to counseling family members of the prisoners and within a year he was doing "full time ministry." God had planted desires deep within him which found their fulfillment when he was simply faithful in small things. But lest we think that serving the Lord always means quitting a secular job to go into ministry "full time," consider the following example.

A young man thought you had to be a minister to serve God. So he exhausted himself trying to hold together a small church in the country. He ended up in a hospital, a very sick and despondent man. But he heard the voice of God asking him, "What do you *really* want to do?" He told God that his real desire was to build houses. God said, "Good, mine too!" He was healed within a week, began a successful construction company, and now gives 70% of his income to missions. Through him Christ builds excellent houses, and he has the respect of all the builders in the state where he lives and works. This man had to leave "the ministry" to find *his* ministry. But for most people it will mean no outward change. It's simply opening our eyes to the white harvest-field where we are.

Jim Elliott, the missionary martyr, said, "Wherever you are, be all there. Live to the hilt every situation you know to be the will of God."[2] There are people whom God has placed in our lives right now whom we need to see with Christ's eyes. There are needs about us for which we need to feel a burden with Christ's compassion. He is seeing these people and feeling that compassion with us. We only need to listen to His commands and obey them. It will be a natural outworking of our own desires.

The Bible teaches that each believer has received spiritual gifts according to the grace given him (Ephesians 4:7–8, 11–13). Many have referred to these abilities as "grace gifts," which accurately explains the word *charismata.* This emphasizes the fact that gifts come from God's free generosity and kindness to us. They are not rewards for good behavior or the result of holiness or maturity. We each have gifts simply because God was good enough to give them to us. Although they are supernatural in origin they are not unnatural in function. A quite natural process can be observed in the function of these gifts. First we observe a need that is unmet—say a group of neighborhood children with nothing to do and no knowledge of God. So we begin to be concerned and burdened for them, and this leads to starting a children's Bible club in the neighborhood. As God blesses this work others begin to recognize that we have a gift for teaching. We humbly recognize that this is all God's doing, even though the whole ministry feels quite natural to us. *We are simply acting according to the prompting of God's Spirit in our inner desires.*

John Stott helpfully points out the difference between salvation and service: "'Saving grace,' the grace which saves sinners, is given to all who believe; but what might be termed 'service grace,' the grace which equips God's people to serve, is given in differing degrees."[3] "Saving grace" is *charis*, and is given to all who have faith. This acceptance of sinners who believe in Christ's sacrifice is the basis of the church's unity. We all are equal at the foot of the cross; we are all in the same ship. Not one of us has earned salvation; we have all received it as a gift. On the other hand, "service grace" or "gifts for serving" is *charismata*, and this is the basis of the church's diversity. By it we are equipped to serve. Here we are *not* equal, because these gifts have been given in differing degrees. "But to each one of us grace was given according to the measure of Christ's gift. . . . He gave gifts to men" (Ephesians

4:7-8). Even though our gifts vary in type and degree, the point is that *each* Christian has received some undeserved ability from Christ to serve his brothers.

The primary problem regarding gifts of the Spirit is a condition you might call "foot-and-hand disease." It is not a fatal condition but it does cause paralysis of ministry. Paul describes it in 1 Corinthians 12 but I would explain it as follows: The "inferior" foot looks at the hand and complains how inferior he is. "Look at all the attention hands get! Folks polish fingernails, put rings on their fingers, and use their hands to greet people. With the hand someone may play a violin, paint a picture, carry out surgery, or throw a touchdown pass. But I'm just a smelly old foot. I'm good for nothing and I don't belong to the body." Just then God interrupts this pity-party and speaks to the foot. "Who takes the musician's hand to the concert hall? Who takes the artist's hand to the studio? Who takes the surgeon's hand to the surgery room? Who takes the quarterback's hand to the football field? Your package of grace may not be as exalted and glorious as that of the hands, but it's just as important."

It is possible to have a healthy view of God and our inner desires and still be paralyzed regarding ministry. A feeling of unworthiness has kept many from being involved in spiritual service. I served for five years on the staff of a parachurch organization and then was invited to work on the pastoral staff of a church. Feelings of inadequacy soon began to mount within. Sure, it was okay to have ministered to college students, I told myself, but this new work was to be in God's church! How could I succeed when I had no Bible training behind me, no seminary education, no knowledge of Greek and Hebrew, no training in counseling or preaching, and no knowledge of church history? It was true that I had lots of practical experience from the campus ministry, but wasn't the church different? Was there a place there for an ex-physical education teacher and campus staff member? Doubts and qualms of inadequacy began to plague me.

It was during this time of of doubt that my family and I rented a cottage for a brief vacation. As I sat on the back porch studying the Book of Amos, God began to speak to me. Amos is an interesting man. He was a layman devoting his life to being a shepherd and a tender of trees. But God gave him a prophetic message and sent him to Bethel to deliver it. Immediately, opposition arose in the person of Bethel's priest who told Amos to get lost. He rejected Amos's message and his person, telling him to "get out." He said that Amos could do his prophesying somewhere else, but not at Bethel. Now Bethel means "house of God" and had been a place of God's presence and blessing. The voice of the enemy in my mind was similar to the voice of this ungodly priest—"You can do your spiritual ministry, but not in the church." To this rejection Amos answered humbly, yet courageously, that he was not a professional prophet and didn't even come from a prophet's family. He confessed to being simply a shepherd and a grower of sycamore figs. But, according to Amos, the Lord took him from that work and said, "Go prophesy" (Amos 7:14).

I left that vacation cottage with a new confidence. I could say, "I am no pastor or even a preacher's kid, I'm simply a physical education teacher and campus staff member. But the Lord took me from training kids in the gym and told me, 'Go pastor people in My church!'" Whether we are qualified or unqualified is not the issue. Hearing the voice of God and obeying it is what counts. Amos may not have been trained for ministry but he certainly heard and responded to God's call.

You may not feel that you have the training or the gifts to be involved in serving the Lord. You may conclude that only those who are gifted can serve God. Well, gifts are wonderful things. The ability to speak or lead or organize are all gifts God bestows on people. If we've received one of these gifts, we have a responsibility to use it. But there is something greater than gifts and it's called grace. John Bunyan, author of *Pilgrim's Progress*, contrasted these two in the following way: "Great grace and small gifts are better than great gifts and no grace."[4] We have all seen extremely gifted people who had none of the grace of God resting upon their lives. Their giftedness burned brightly like a piece of paper thrown into a fireplace. It flashed brilliantly for a few moments and called attention to itself, but soon went out without having warmed the room. Far better is the little-gifted person who has great grace empowering his efforts. He burns steadily like a hardwood log. People of this type are the true builders of the kingdom of God. Great grace and small gifts is God's plan for most of His servants.

Eric Liddell exemplifies this principle beautifully. Most of the movie "Chariots of Fire" focuses on his gold medal in the 1925 Olympics and his uncompromising conviction. But the real story of his life is what happened after that success. He had little speaking ability, yet his messages were used of God to move thousands in Scotland toward the Lord. This was not simply the popularity of a national hero but the anointing of God. Later, as a missionary to China, he continued to excel until his early death from a brain tumor. At his memorial service the following testimonials to his life were given: "He was not particularly clever, and not conspicuously able, but he was good. . . . He wasn't a great leader, or an inspired thinker, but he knew what he ought to do, and he did it. . . . I say that Eric is the most remarkable example in my experience of a man of average ability developing those talents to an amazing degree. . . . He was literally God-controlled, in his thoughts, judgments, actions, and words to an extent I have never seen surpassed and rarely seen equalled."[5] Eric Liddell is a model of small gifts and great grace.

Life was meant to be an *adventure*. We can live

self-indulgently . . . and spend our lives meandering down the predictable road called "Boredom." It's a life without the fizz in the pop. Or we can serve and meet the needs of others . . . on the road called "Adventure." This is the way to an exciting life. *Grace* plants the desire in me to serve and opens my eyes to see the needs about me. Grace also equips me with any gift I may need. And grace is even able to overrule any ungiftedness and bless my feeble efforts to love and serve people. The grace-life is a life of surprises and adventures! God says that He has planned out a pattern of good works for us to walk in. They have already been set up and we have only to discover and enjoy them. We can begin each morning and say, "Lord, I'm excited to find out what you've planned for us to do together today. I'm available, so let's get started."

Lack of training, lack of gifts, uncertainty about God's will, and distrust of inner desires all can work together to paralyze us for spiritual ministry. But God's grace frees and liberates us to move into *action*. Grace accepts people who are undertrained and uses people who make mistakes. God's grace working through average people like you and me is accomplishing *far more good* in this world than all of man's fancy technology and brilliant superstars! God's weakness is *stronger* than man's strength! So let's move into action, confident of the fact that God in us is able and adequate for anything we'll have to face. There is nothing passive about the Spirit-led person. Life for him has become what it was supposed to be: an adventure filled with surprises, fun, seriousness, caring, purpose, and deep inner joyfulness. By the energy of *grace* the fizz can once again be in the pop!

CHAPTER 12

GRACE AND FINANCIAL BLESSING

Bill's favorite TV preacher was on today and was talking about money. The evangelist had mentioned the subject often, but today the message really got through to Bill. "God wants you to be rich! Poverty, need, sickness and lack are all part of the fall, and from the devil. Abundance, health and prosperity are the inherited possessions of God's children. If you follow Jesus, He will lead you out of want and need into a life of abundance. It's yours to claim by faith."

Bill had heard it all many times before. It was this positive message that drew him to the evangelist in the first place. But today's sermon came home with real application. The "how to" of this prosperity was simply to visualize his financial success and it would become a reality. Since high school he had determined to make a million dollars by age 35. Now he had the tools and the blessing of God to go with it. He committed himself with new resolve to pursue his goals.

How would Bill evaluate whether or not God had been gracious to him? According to his theology, the answer was clear cut. The ones with the most grace are identified by the cars they drive, the clothes they wear, the houses they live in and the vacations they go on. It's best expressed by the popular slogan: "The one with the most toys wins." If Bill attained his chunk of the good life, then he had experienced God's grace.

But we need to ask some questions about this theology. Is it possible that Bill is hearing false teaching? Is it possible that he is simply pasting a spiritual veneer over a worldly ambition? Is it possible that he is actually living his life under the leadership of the "spirit of the age" rather than the Spirit of God?

The pursuit of wealth and prosperity is on the minds of millions of Americans. But the origin of this mind-set is not with the TV preacher. There is another, far-more-effective preacher who planted the thought to begin with. This preacher does not have a weekly broadcast and he does not mail out literature. He is probably the most effective preacher of the prosperity message in America today and his name is the devil. Sometimes he appears in sheep's clothing and quotes the Bible, but he also uses many other forms to preach his message.

What's wrong with wanting to be rich? Listen to God's perspective as He warns against the dangers of seeking wealth: "The man who wants to be rich will have eight problems: he will be tempted to sin, he will fall unknowingly into a trap, foolish desires will master him, harmful desires will eat away at his character, he will be plunged into moral ruin, his desire for wealth will be his destruction, he will wander from the faith, and many griefs will pierce his soul" (1 Timothy 6:9–10, paraphrased). That's an interesting way to describe what everyone in our society seems to be dreaming and longing for! It gives a side of the picture not seen on "Lifestyles of the Rich and Famous." And it's certainly not what Bill had in mind when he set out to be a millionaire!

As we consider the above warning, we know that this does not mean that it's sinful to *be* rich. After all, Job, Abraham, and David were all rich and godly at the same time. Rather, it's a warning against the dangers of wanting to *become* rich. The danger is not in *possessing* wealth (although that has its problems), but in being so eager for money that you make it a *god* in your life. Bill had crossed over that line and made wealth and its pursuit the deity of his life. He would disguise this ambition with biblical phrases; but that wouldn't change the fact that prosperity had become an idol he worshiped. He was living by worldly motivation while calling it spiritual.

In coming out against today's prosperity gospel it's possible to swing too far the other way and miss the biblical balance. Although we are commanded not to worship money, neither are we to glorify poverty. Although the benefits of following Christ are spiritual, they are also material. The golden word "balance" is often missed as the pendulum swings from one side to the other. In reacting against the prosperity teachers, we must not reject perfectly scriptural promises simply because they happen to be about the material realm.

For instance, we are told that "God shall supply all your needs according to His riches" (Philippians 4:19). The context is financial. We are told that God will "open for you the windows of heaven, and pour out for you a blessing until it overflows" (Malachi 3:10). The context is financial. We are instructed to "Honor the Lord from your wealth, and from the first of all your produce; so your barns will be filled with plenty, and your vats will overflow with new wine" (Proverbs 3:9-10). To ignore such promises is simply reactionary and does not take into account the whole council of God on the subject of finances. Poverty is not glorified in the Scriptures. Wesley lamented over his poor converts, "How can I prevent those lately converted to Christ from becoming wealthy? The wasteful become frugal, diligence replaces sloth, and the selfish become loving. How can such people remain poor and indigent?"[1]

The issue is not whether one is poor or wealthy or somewhere in between. When God's grace invades our finances we automatically become generous. The key word is not *prosperity* but *generosity*. Here is how Paul said grace would affect the Corinthians' finances: "And God is able to make all grace abound to you, so that in all things at all times, having all that you need, you will abound in every good work. . . . You will be made rich in every way so that you can be generous on every occasion (2 Corinthians 9:8–11 *NIV*). Abounding grace leads to abounding generosity. The gift the Corinthians were supposed to offer to the poverty-stricken church at Jerusalem could itself be called the grace (*charis*) of God (1 Corinthians 16:3). Paul concludes by saying that when the Corinthians demonstrate their generosity, then others will see the "surpassing grace of God" that has been given to them (2 Corinthians 9:14).

When God's grace is upon our finances, two conditions usually follow: First, all our needs will be met and we will probably be better off. Second, we will gain a generous spirit. By grace we'll usually take more money in and will definitely send more money out. This is radically different from worldly goals. Those in the world are seeking *wealth* to increase their affluent lifestyle; those in Christ are seeking *grace* to have their needs met and increase their generosity. It would seem like the whole world is standing in line waiting to purchase their lottery ticket in the hope of becoming rich. Their dreams are all focused upon that fantasy day when they strike it rich. Meanwhile, the followers of Christ are busy living life to the fullest, debt free, needs met, and making others rich along the way.

This principle of generosity can be true regardless of one's financial state. Consider the example of someone without material resources. A friend came to the United States from Romania and the Lord has been good to him. His brother is still in Romania, and was living in poverty with his seven children. Romania was under Communist rule and the gospel was not allowed to go in or out of that country. Several years ago my friend, George, sent his brother $100 through a friend who was traveling to his homeland on vacation. But when George's brother was given the money, he refused to accept it even though it was equivalent to a month's wages and was much needed.

His message in returning the money was as follows: "Tell George to give it to missions. We have no way to help missionaries here, so I want it to be used in this way and speed the return of Christ." This man was so concerned for the spiritually lost of the world that even in his poverty he delighted to use 100% of this gift for missionary outreach! Every time George sits down to a good meal, he remembers his brother living sacrificially for the Lord in Romania. There are still those who are suffering for the gospel. There are still those who, like the Macedonians, are begging for the opportunity to give money for the Lord's work. In describing the poverty and generosity of these believers, Paul says, "We wish to make known to you the grace of God which has been given in the churches of Macedonia" (2 Corinthians 8:1). Their joy came not from driving around in Macedonian Mercedeses or cruising in the Mediterranean.

Rather, they rejoiced in their generosity even as believers in Romania are doing today. The Macedonian spirit is still alive. God's grace may not make everyone prosperous, but it *will* always make us generous. Paul describes himself as "poor yet making many rich, as having nothing yet possessing all things" (2 Corinthians 6:10).

The other side of the coin is wealth. The Scriptures shows us that it's possible to be both wealthy and generous at the same time. Rich Abraham gave a tenth to Melchizedek (Genesis 14:20). In the New Testament, we see some apparently wealthy women who contributed to the parasynagogue ministry of Jesus (Luke 8:3). They must have experienced great fulfillment in knowing that their gifts were being used by Christ to establish the kingdom of God. I have known a number of Christians who were materially quite wealthy, yet they developed and maintained wonderful giving hearts. By God's grace may the number of this "tribe" increase greatly, because they will be used of the Lord to expand the kingdom of light in this world of darkness.

Man's religion usually comes up with the wrong answers to the problems of life. Teaching tends to polarize around the extremes of prosperity and poverty. Frequently the wealthy are made to feel guilty because they have more than others. Judgmental religion looks at these folks with a critical eye and concludes they must be materialistic—forgetting that God is the one who gives people the ability to produce wealth (Deuteronomy 8:18). Grace simply says to those rich in this present world: "Be grateful! Be generous!" No condemnation, no judgment. Just simple Christian living. Rather than being made to feel guilty, the rich are urged to realize that it is God who "richly supplies us with all things to enjoy" and to add to their material wealth the spiritual riches of good deeds (1 Timothy 6:17–18). The balanced message of the Scriptures to the upper middle class is not a ticket to go on a "guilt trip." Rather, it's an encouragement to enjoy gratefully the good they have and a challenge to sign up for a "service trip," thus making the greatest joy of their life doing good and sharing their abundance with others.

On the other side of the scale are those desiring to be rich. The religionist looks down on them, saying that if they "only had enough faith" they'd be wealthy. But grace simply says, "Be content!" (1 Timothy 6:6–8). Again, no condemnation for the financial status they find themselves in. The Apostle Paul said, "I have learned to be content in whatever circumstances I am" (Philippians 4:11). He knew how to live with prosperity as well as humble means, and realized that neither state was a reflection of his spiritual life. Yet it is generally true that following Christ, as Wesley pointed out, will inevitably help a person to become more prosperous. He will work harder, stay out of debt, tithe his income, give to the poor, and practice many other biblical principles that will help him financially.

But his actions will spring from a motive of contented obedience rather than material greed.

There is one final application of grace to our finances and it has to do with the incarnation. Paul explains it dramatically: "For you know the grace of our Lord Jesus Christ, that though he was rich, yet for your sakes he became poor, so that you through his poverty might become rich" (2 Corinthians 8:9 *NIV*). Through the self-emptying grace of Christ, all believers have become fabulously wealthy. His poverty brings us the riches of generosity, contentment, inner peace, and sometimes material blessings. We become rich in forgiveness, love, spiritual power, and the wisdom which comes from the wonderful Book God has given to us. As David said, "The law of Thy mouth is better to me than thousands of gold and silver pieces" (Psalms 119:72). But most importantly, we gain the infinite, unsearchable riches of the Son of God living His life in and through our finite selves. These are the true riches!

A number of years ago, I had an experience that illustrates what I've been trying to say in this chapter. I was speaking at a small black college where the students were quite poor. After the meeting they gave me an offering which I tried to refuse, but they insisted that I accept. The girl presenting the offering told this story. She worked as a cleaning lady for a wealthy woman. But most of her friends were poor like herself. At that point in her life she was much in need of clothing, yet she distinctly heard God's voice telling her to give one of her few dresses to a friend. How could God require this of her? But after several days of arguing with God, she yielded and cheerfully gave the dress to her friend. The following week the lady whose house she cleaned informed her that she was getting a whole new wardrobe and she could have all the dresses in the closet. They were virtually new, and all fit perfectly.

As she told me this story, she closed her fist tightly and said that if we hold on to what we have, we aren't open to receive from God. Then she opened her hand and said if we are free to let go of what we have, we will also be able to receive what the Lord has to give. Such is the way the grace of God works in our lives. *Grace motivates us to live a life of generosity and increases our ability to receive from a giving God.* I've never forgotten that girl and her story of God's faithfulness. It's a picture of God's grace in action. She seemed to be greatly blessed in giving that gift to me and I could see she was really a cheerful giver. But I was also blessed in receiving this gift. It taught me a lesson about graciously receiving gifts of love from people who are really sacrificing to give. When God's grace gets involved in finances, it usually brings joy to both giver and receiver.

CHAPTER 13

GRACE AND PERSONAL FREEDOM

Everyone wants to be free. One of the greatest benefits of living under grace is the personal freedom it brings to us. However, this freedom is probably one of the least understood aspects of God's grace. To grasp the meaning of becoming free we need to understand some basic concepts found in the Book of Galatians.

The first concept is that before a person exercises faith in the Lord Jesus he is *tightly locked inside the prison of the law.* "Before this faith came, we were held prisoners by the law, locked up until faith [in the finished work of Christ] should be revealed" (Galatians 3:23 *NIV*).

Use your imagination for a moment and let me tell you a story that illustrates this truth. Rod has been behind bars for as long as he can remember. Prison has become a way of life for him. But like everyone else, he wants to get out and live as a free man. In our little story there *is* a way to get out— and that is never to break the rules! If you break one

rule, your time is immediately extended to a life
sentence. But even though perfection is the only
way out, most of the prisoners, including Rod, are
under the impression that if they are kind to each
other and just do the best they can, some day they
will be released. Yet there is no evidence that
anyone has ever gotten out by this method.

Rod was amazed at the sheer size of the prison
population. It seemed to be growing each day,
while he personally did not know anyone who had
ever been released. His determination to get out
was enormous. Day after day he worked and
labored to be a better person. He had now pro-
gressed beyond simply conquering his vices and
was attempting to practice various virtues. Yet the
more he tried to be good, the worse he knew
himself to be. When he was young, he would
sometimes go to the prison gates and shake them.
They seemed fairly loose. But now, after all these
efforts to keep the rules, it seemed that in some
strange way the prison gates were actually getting
tighter and more secure. At the same time, he was
recognizing how fully he broke many rules, not just
in letter but also in spirit. The better he became
outwardly, the worse he knew himself to be inwardly!

Occasionally outsiders came into the prison for
special meetings. Today was such a day, and Rod
was unusually interested in hearing the free people
speak. They sang joyful freedom songs, gave testi-
monies about the outside world, and taught about

the Liberator at these get-togethers. Today's talk was about a second way to get out of the prison. They said that the "keep the rules" method just didn't work, but that one had come into prison from outside, kept all the rules, and then gave Himself to be executed in place of others. Through trusting this Liberator a prisoner would receive a card with "Grace" on one side and "Pardoned" on the other side. It was said that this card would open the prison gate.

Rod was interested. After the meeting, he talked with one of the free people and put his faith in the Liberator. He was immediately given one of the cards, which to his great joy opened the prison gate as soon as he thrust it into the slot. As he breathed the fresh air of the outside world, he knew why all the free people did so much singing. The most amazing thing to Rod was the contrast between all his vain efforts to open the gate and the instantly effective card which led to his release. The change in his thought-life was truly amazing. He used to be overwhelmed with fearful thoughts that he was too sinful ever to be released. Now he knew all men were rule breakers, including himself, and that no one could secure their own release. In his mind he constantly returned to this wonderful card he had been given and the beautiful words which were printed on it. Previously he had tried to keep the rules in desperate hope of escaping the prison. Now, with absolutely no thought or effort in regard to the rules, he was a free man, free from an ineffective system and free from his desperate confinement. It was as if a thousand-pound weight had been removed from his shoulders.

We will pause in our little story about Rod to make some observations. In a very simple way the story is telling us that the law keeps us in bondage until Christ comes to us. In fact, it's the prison of the law that makes freedom in Christ look so desirable. Only through faith in Him can we be liberated from the oppressive custody that the law has kept us under. The emancipation that Rod is now experiencing is primarily *freedom from the bondage of the law*. Rod's conscience has been set free from the guilt of sin! People, both inside and outside of the prison, break the rules. But those inside are trying to know God through rule-keeping and those outside know God through faith in the finished work of Christ, their Liberator.

Those inside feel the weight of guilt pressing upon them but those outside are free from the guilt of sin. Those inside are working feverishly to counteract, somehow, their lawless deeds with good ones. Those outside the prison are trusting confidently that Christ has honored their faith and made them acceptable.

Probably one of the most noted "prisoners" ever to be released was Martin Luther. He was a man overwhelmed by guilt and led by law to plunge himself vainly into penances, mortifications, and all kinds of religious rituals and self-denials. Yet none of these good works soothed his conscience.

Finally, in despair, he was led to discover a salvation *based on grace*. This way out of guilt was offered as a free gift in response to simple faith. As this one man received the gift, he discovered what freedom was all about! We might say he received the "Grace" card and then began to write about it and preach about it and testify about it and even sing about it. Soon thousands had an identical card in their possession, and the result was what we call the Reformation.

But let's return to our story now. Rod has been enjoying the land of liberation tremendously. He is finding great companionship with other free men and is even making occasional trips back to the prison to give testimony for the Liberator. But it's at this point that he observes two strange happenings among the free people in the land of liberation. The first is a movement of free people back to the prison. They are not going in to give testimony but rather to be locked up again inside the confines of the prison! They are returning to the old system of rule-keeping in order to gain freedom! They are walking away from freedom and back to bondage and imprisonment. The second happening Rod observed among some free people was equally strange. Many of them were biting each other on the face and arms in open hostility. You could tell these folks by the open wounds on their bodies. They had none of the joy of their fellow free men. The situation puzzled Rod greatly. One group returning to their bondage . . . and the other blatantly breaking all the rules they could think of and hurting one another in the process.

Rod began to take a survey of both groups to discover their motivation. He found that those who were lined up seeking voluntary imprisonment all felt a lack of confidence in the "Grace" card they had received. In fact, many of them had even forgotten that it was in their possession. They had become aware of some of their continued rule-breaking as free men and had concluded they were unworthy of the land of liberation. So they were moving back to the prison to establish their own goodness. They were going back to the thought-patterns they had lived with for so many years. The second group, those involved in the biting, had a different problem. Rod discovered that to a man they all misunderstood their freedom. Every one of these liberated people thought they had not only been set free in conscience, but also from controls. They thought they were set free *to* sin, not *from* sin. So they indulged all their sinful desires, even if it led to hurting their brothers. Just like the first group, they also became prisoners again—not to the prison house of the law but to their own passions. Rod determined that he would spend the rest of his days helping these once-liberated people to recover the freedom they once had. And with that we end our parable.

Both of these groups existed in the first-century church. The Apostle Paul was raised up by God not only to preach the gospel of God's grace to the *lost*, but also to establish *believers* in their position of grace. Paul's cry to the poor folks heading back toward prison would be the strong words found in his letter to the Galatians: "It was for freedom that Christ set us free; therefore keep standing firm and do not be subject again to a yoke of slavery" (Galatians 5:1). The way a man stands firm in his freedom is to resist the thought that he is accepted by God because of his merit. A voice may be heard in our minds that says, "You've had some slip-ups this week. You've broken some of My laws. You know I don't like you quite as much now. You'd better get to work and shape up so that I will love and accept you once more." These thoughts must be rejected as a slander on the character of God. There is nothing humble or noble about such ideas. They are heresy! On the basis of grace, God gives us free and total forgiveness in Christ. We have His love and acceptance in its fullness, totally apart from our performance or any merit of our own once we've put our faith in Christ.

If we are going to live a life based on grace, then we must live *as free men!* The Christian life is not one of slavery, confinement or bondage, but of freedom. We are free to believe that God *totally* and *completely* accepts us, based on the sacrifice of His Son. It is a sad fact that many who attend Protestant churches—churches founded on the principles Martin Luther discovered in Scripture—know nothing of the liberty that he experienced. Regardless of our church affiliation, let *us* rediscover the Liberator and allow Him to burst open the prison doors of our own lives and lead us into the land of free grace! We must not return to the prison!

But Paul would also have some words for the second group, that violent bunch who were biting each other. Perhaps when you first read that you thought, "How grotesque!" Well, you're right. But it's the same picture Paul painted for us in Galatians. "Do not turn your freedom into an opportunity for the flesh. . . . If you bite and devour one another, take care lest you be consumed by one another" (Galatians 5:13-15). Christ set us free from a guilty conscience and a human merit mindset; but He didn't free us from all moral constraints. We have total liberty to draw close to God, but we don't have total liberty to draw close to sin. To throw out all moral restraint is to build *your own* prison house.

A modern person says, "I'm free to take drugs." Our answer is, Yes, you have that choice—but the so-called "freedom" will make you a slave to chemicals. Now you *must* have your drugs. You have no choice. You're a prisoner to your own sin. And the same is true of the more "respectable" sins such as gossip, slander, or criticism. If we claim to be free to do these, we enter into a cruel form of slavery and bondage. We find ourselves acting like animals, fighting and biting each other. That is *not* freedom.

So what is the solution? If going back to the prison house of the law is wrong and if throwing out all moral restraints is wrong, then what are we to do? How can we both stay free and live godly? The answer is found in one word: Love! When our two boys were young and my wife and I had Bible studies with them, they would sometimes answer every question we asked with one stock answer, "Love." If they didn't know the answer to the question, that's the answer they'd give, and nine times out of ten it would be correct. Now how does *love* answer the above question?

The false teachers saw circumcision as symbolic of the doctrine of good works. But when Paul discusses it, he declares circumcision valueless. Instead there is only one thing that matters and that is "faith expressing itself through love" (Galatians 5:6 *NIV*). This solves the dilemma. Faith keeps us out of the prison house of the law. If it's true saving faith, it will lead to love! And love keeps us from biting and devouring each other. In fact, if we love we will end up fulfilling the whole law (Galatians 5:14). If we truly love, we won't murder or commit adultery or steal or be coveters or bear false witness. Modern thinking throws out all absolutes and says you're free to do whatever you like; biblical thinking embraces the law of love and leads us to live by absolutes in our personal conduct. As John Stott has so helpfully written: "We must notice carefully what the apostle writes. He does not say, as some of the 'new moralists' are saying, that if we love one another we can safely *break* the law in the interests of love; but [he is saying] that if we love one another we shall *fulfill* the law, because the whole law is summed up in this one command, 'You shall love your neighbor as yourself.'"[1]

So my boys were right. The answer *is* love (as it usually is to most of the big questions). In fact, there is an unusual paradox here. True love will lead us to serve God and to serve men. Paul says, "Do not turn your freedom into an opportunity for the flesh, but through love serve one another" (Galatians 5:13). The word he uses for *serve* really means "to be a slave." Christian freedom involves this idea of being a love-slave to the Lord and to people. And in this slavery is great freedom. In the Book of Exodus we are told of the slave who is offered freedom but declines it because of his love for the master. He would then have his ear lobe pierced and voluntarily become a servant for life. Consider the hymn, "My Glorious Victor, Prince Divine" by Handley Moule:

> My Master, lead me to Thy door; pierce this now
>   willing ear once more;
> Thy bonds are freedom; let me stay with Thee, to toil,
>   endure, obey.
> Yes, ear and hand and thought and will — use all in
>   Thy dear slav'ry still!
> Self's weary liberties I cast beneath Thy feet; there
>   keep them fast.

This then is the two-fold freedom that *grace* qualifies us to experience. First of all, it is a freedom from the law and that terrible feeling of not measuring up. Believers are people who have stepped outside of the prison house that the whole world is confined in; they are breathing the sweet air of grace, and have confidence that God totally and completely accepts them. They are *free to draw near to God!* And secondly, Christian freedom is liberty to love. As people who know with certainty that they are going to heaven, we are *free to love and serve others along the way.* So faith expressing itself through love solves the dilemma and gives us true freedom! Faith sets us free from the law's cruel bondage and love protects us from the unrestrained passions of the flesh.

An eleven-year-old boy joined his father to begin life as a seaman. His early life became a steady flow of self-indulgence and rebellion. Eventually this young man became a captain of his own ship. The business: capturing, transporting, and selling black slaves from Africa to the West Indies and America. He lived a cruel and degrading life. But on March 10, 1748, in the midst of an extremely stormy voyage where it looked like they would all lose their lives, John Newton began to seek God. He eventually accepted Christ and was converted, leaving the ugly slave trade behind him. But personal spiritual freedom did not leave him a private, selfish individual. He crusaded against slavery and eventually became ordained to the ministry in the Anglican Church.

John Newton's preaching influenced many, in-

cluding the great anti-slavery crusader William
Wilberforce. Newton died in 1807, and in that same
year the British Parliament abolished slavery in its
entire domain. Newton's tombstone has this in-
scription, written by himself: "John Newton, clerk,
once an infidel and libertine, a servant of slaves in
Africa, was by the rich mercy of our Lord and
Savior Jesus Christ, preserved, restored, pardoned
and appointed to preach the faith he had long
labored to destroy."[2] But perhaps the greatest influence this once slave-maker turned slave-libera-
tor has had upon our lives is the hymn he penned
after experiencing his own spiritual emancipation:

Amazing grace—how sweet the sound—that saved a
    wretch like me!
I once was lost, but now am found—was blind, but now
    I see.

'Twas grace that taught my heart to fear, and grace
    my fears relieved;
How precious did that grace appear the hour I first
    believed!

Through many dangers, toils and snares I have already
    come;
'Tis grace has brought me safe thus far and grace will
    lead me home.

The Lord has promised good to me: His word my hope
    secures;
He will my shield and portion be as long as life endures.

And when this flesh and heart shall fail, and mortal life
    shall cease,
I shall possess within the veil a life of joy and peace.

When we've been there ten thousand years, bright
    shining as the sun,
We've no less days to sing God's praise than when we'd
    first begun.

CHAPTER 14

KEEPING THE CHANNELS OPEN

Some people experience more of God's grace than others. At differing points in each of our lives we experience more of God's grace than at other times. Both of these truths point to the fact that God's grace is not static but dynamic, not regulated by a rigid formula but living, moving, and changing. I have experienced times when outwardly I was doing everything right, yet there was no sense of God's presence, blessing, and anointing on my activities. At other times I've made one mistake after another and keenly felt all my weaknesses operating at full speed, and yet the hand of God was upon me for good.

Yet, saying that grace is dynamic and not static is not to say that it is unpredictable or unexplainable. In a few moments we will examine the means of grace and the key to its flow in our lives. These two factors explain much of the working of grace. But before we look at those principles, we should grasp the significance the writers of Scripture give to the word "grace."

In the New Testament we are told that salvation is all by God's grace. We are chosen and called by grace, and we are saved, justified, and forgiven by it. When we get to heaven we will find no one boastfully strutting around and bragging about what he did to get there. Rather, all who enter those gates will be exalting *grace* and testifying to what *God* has done for them. Salvation is all of grace. And not only is this true of our salvation, but also our sanctification. We are told to *grow* in grace, *be strong* in it, *stand* in it, *hope* in it, *serve* in it, and *be established* in it. In short, sanctification is all of grace also.

Paul's major doctrinal epistle, the Book of Romans, speaks of grace over twenty times. It is clearly a major thread woven into his view of the Christian life. At a point of climax in his argument he asserts that those who take into their hearts the abundance of grace will actually reign and rule in life. They will be on top of the waves, master of the storms, and conqueror over all the fierce gales of affliction. The banner waving from the mast of their ship will say, "King Grace reigns supreme!!" (Romans 5:17, 21).

It is this passage of Scripture which was largely responsible for the Welsh revival of 1904, and it is this truth that will usher in personal revival in each of our lives. God's righteousness through God's grace makes fearful seamen into conquering captains. We can take authority over the storms of life.

Romans teaches us that we can reign through

never run out. God has *incomparable riches* of grace and out of that rich treasure house He has *lavished* this grace upon us. God is extravagantly generous and liberal in His giving.   More than we deserve and more than we need is His abundant supply. The Book of Acts tells us that "great grace" was upon all of the believers. But this does not seem to be true of the church today. Not all have great grace upon them.

Why does it appear that some people have more of God's grace upon their lives than others? If God is so rich in His abundant grace, as we observed at the beginning of this study, then why do some people seemingly trudge through life struggling to make it on their own without the help of God's grace? The answer to these questions is the key to the free flow of God's grace into our lives. It is also the type of key that we must keep using repeatedly if the channels are to be kept open. What is that key?

Before we examine that "key," we must look at a practice which has been referred to by theologians as a "means of grace." But first, let us answer the preliminary question, What are the means of grace? Theologians speak of several different "means of grace" through which the Holy Spirit works. Included are the proclamation and hearing of the Word of God, partaking of the sacraments (baptism and the Lord's supper), church membership, corporate Christian fellowship, personal Bible study and prayer.

I wish to zero in on the last two "means" just

I wish to zero in on the last two "means" just mentioned, i.e., Bible study and prayer. Considered as a unit, in some quarters this is referred to as the "daily quiet time."

Taking time each day for personal Bible study and prayer make up the mechanics of having a quiet time. But beneath the mechanics there is to be a deep desire to know, obey, and be conformed personally to the Lord Jesus Christ. It has been referred to by some as having a "personal passion for Christ." It is a strong, driving conviction that for me *really* to live *is* Christ. If I can't know Him intimately, and if His presence cannot go with me, life becomes meaningless. To seek Him and see His face becomes the holy obsession of my life.

So we study our Bibles each day and through the Spirit of Truth we hear God's voice speaking. He convicts us of our shortcomings. He guides our decisions. He strengthens our faith. But above all, He shows us Christ. We learn to worship and pray. We talk to God daily about our problems, our joys, our confusion, and our anger. It's not a legalistic duty that I must do in order to conform to a certain Christian sub-culture. Rather, the daily quiet time is the magnificent privilege of having a one-on-one counseling session with the greatest of all Counselors. It is receiving my marching orders for the day directly from the King of kings. It is communing through love letters with the Lover of my soul. *That* is Bible study and prayer, and it is very accurate to refer to these two practices as means of grace.

God's grace certainly does flow through these channels. If you have not established a "quiet time" in your daily routine, then I urge you to do so today. Make a lifelong policy decision that you will meet with God each day in worshipful prayer and seek His face through study of the Scriptures. It may be only 10–15 minutes each morning, but you will find that it will be the most significant time of your whole day. It will be one of the most significant decision of your whole life. I was introduced to the daily quiet time by staff and students of Inter-Varsity Christian Fellowship the first year I became a Christian. I have never regretted pursuing it.

But having said all of this about this "means of grace," it must be added that a quiet time is not the key to receiving more grace into our lives. Bible study and prayer are certainly valuable as a means of grace but they are not the *key* to grace. There is one character quality which represents this key; one attitude of heart which determines how much of God's grace we experience, by whatever channel; one outlook which is the *golden virtue* leading to God's grace. It is the virtue of *humility!* The simple ability of humbling ourselves is the key to unlocking and releasing the flow of God's grace.

Humility increases grace in our lives. Its opposite, pride, will hinder and decrease the flow of grace. Strangely, the more grace we experience in our lives, the more we are tempted to abandon grace. The better things go, the more success we see, the more fruit we bear, the stronger is the temptation to attribute the prosperity to self and not to God. James tells us that God sets Himself in active opposition against the proud man, but the humble person will experience increasing gifts of "more grace" given to him. Pride and humility are something like the hot and cold water faucets in your sink. They determine *what* will flow and *how much* will flow.

It is possible, even predictable, for a man to walk with God for years and grow in power and influence within God's kingdom, only to become cold, hard, and unteachable in his later years. Samuel challenged King Saul with these tragic words, "Although you were once small in your own eyes, did you not become the head of the tribes of Israel?" (1 Samuel 15:17 *NIV*). Saul allowed pride to enter his life, inflating his ego and hardening his heart. The flow of God's grace dried up as he defended wrong decisions, refused to accept rebuke, and would not learn from correction. Apart from the Spirit, this is the natural sin-pattern that great men slide into when humility ceases to be important to them.

But David, unlike Saul, maintained his teachableness even after he saw fantastic success. David was far from perfect. But when Nathan the prophet rebuked him, he humbled himself immediately with the only appropriate words, "I have sinned." After being pelted with stones during the Absalom affair, David received the rebuke and upon his return to Jerusalem said of the stone thrower, "Leave him alone. God told him to curse me." A third incident further demonstrates Israel's greatest king's humility. After bullheadedly going against the advice of his counselors and having his fighting men numbered—demonstrating a reliance on his own resources rather than showing the naked faith he had exercised in confronting Goliath years before—when the report finally came in nine months later, David was conscience stricken with his failure and again humbled himself in confession. He was a man with numerous failings; yet he practiced great humility in not defending or justifying his wrong actions. It is no wonder God's grace was upon him.

John Stott says that there is something obscene and offensive about pride, something calculated to disgust. He warns of pride's subtle, insidious nature. It is possible for men to take on an outward demeanor of great meekness while, within, their appetite for applause is insatiable. Baxter is quoted as saying, "O what a constant companion, what a tyrannical commander, what a sly and insinuating enemy is this sin of pride."[1]

Peter tells us to humble ourselves under God's mighty hand and the result will be God lifting us rather than opposing us. There is a difference between humbling ourselves and being humbled by circumstances. Too often we fail to bend our own knees so they must be bent by the Lord. Alan Redpath, the former pastor of Moody Church, shared a personal experience he had with God's chastening hand in 1964. He suffered a cerebral hemorrhage which left him devastated—physically, mentally, and spiritually. He sank into depths of despair which were beyond description. Sinful thoughts, temptations to impurity, bad language and other problems that he hadn't wrestled with for over twenty years were now his daily conflict. After weeks of darkness he came to a place of complete despair and asked God to deliver him from these attacks of the devil and take him home.

At that moment, for the first time in months, God seemed to draw near to him. A deep conviction of God's voice come to his heart, saying, "You have this all wrong. The devil has nothing to do with it. It is I, your Savior, who has brought this experience into your life to show you two things.

"First, this is the kind of person—with all your sinful thoughts and temptations, which you thought were things of the past—that you *always* will be, *but for my grace*. I have never intended to make you a 'better man.' In the second place, I want to replace you with Myself, if you will only allow Me to be God in you, and admit that you are a complete failure, and that the only good thing about Alan Redpath is *Jesus*."[2] He had known and preached this truth as theory for some years. Now he knew it by experience. From that day forward he lived that truth out in a totally new way.

Outward success can often make a man feel proud and self-confident. One can forget that his strength, gifts, and fruitfulness have all come from

God. Redpath's testimony reminds us that apart from Christ we are nothing. When prosperity is accompanied by pride it will cut off the flow of God's grace. The outward momentum of success may continue but the inner sense of God's presence, power, and glory will vanish. Without God's grace we are no better and no more useful than we were in our unredeemed state.

For grace to flow freely, we need this settled conviction that the only good thing about me is Jesus. The only thing spiritual or holy about me is the life of Christ. With this conviction, we will be protected from pride in times of success. From this conviction, that Christ *alone* is my righteousness and goodness, springs an ever-deepening experience with God's grace. A. W. Tozer summarized it beautifully in one of his prayers: "O God, I have tasted Thy goodness and it has both satisfied me and made me thirsty for more. I am painfully conscious of my need for further grace. I am ashamed of my lack of desire. O God, the Triune God, I want to want Thee, I long to be filled with longing. I thirst to be made more thirsty still."[3]

Only as we maintain this attitude of brokenness, humility, and desire will the flow of God's grace remain strong. As we humble ourselves in this way, we will see God fulfilling His promise that He "is opposed to the proud, but gives grace to the humble" (James 4:6). It takes courage to be honest with ourselves. It is often painful and difficult to face up to our weaknesses and acknowledge our dependence. It takes a careful examining of our hearts to see that *His* attitude is maintained. But when we walk humbly with our God, we will know that we've found the way. We will not be like Christian in the dungeon, in *Pilgrim's Progress*, who forgot that the key was hanging around his neck all the time. We will use the key often and see the mighty Niagara of God's grace flow in its fullness into every corner of our lives. humility

From the foothills of Miletus one could look down upon the beautiful Mediterranean port below. On the beach ten or fifteen men were gathered in a tight little group. A ship ready to sail off was anchored in the bay while a small boat was pulled up on the shore, waiting to taxi a passenger out to the ship. The men were all leaders from a young church in a nearby city. A short, unimpressive-looking Jewish man has been talking to them, obviously with deep emotion. As we approach the group, we hear the speaker saying that his friends will never see his face again. Tears are streaming down their faces as they kneel in the sand together in a farewell prayer.

The young church leaders are probably unaware that the man they are praying with is one of the greatest minds of all history. They are probably unaware that he is the greatest theologian, missionary, and church planter the world will ever see. They would not know that nineteen hundred years later men from every corner of the earth would be studying, analyzing, and obeying his written letters. All they knew was that they loved the man very much, and that he had impacted their lives as no other. What would his closing words be? What last thought would he leave with them? He spoke quietly but with deep confidence and conviction, "Now I commend you to God and to the word of His grace, which is able to build you up and to give you the inheritance among all those who are sanctified" (Acts 20:32). He placed them in the care and protection of God and His grace. He gave them into the keeping of the most powerful force on earth, a force that could both strengthen and enrich them.

Simple words—but deeply profound. Words that said it all in one short sentence. The whole provision of heaven and the whole need of man in two words: God's grace. As the great Apostle Paul climbed into the boat that would carry him on his continued mission of "testifying to the gospel of the grace of God," he was confident that his friends were securely in the good ship *Grace*.

NOTES

Dedication page:

1. Bruce, F.F. *The Epistle of Paul to the Romans* (Tyndale New Testament Commentaries), Grand Rapids, MI: Wm. B. Eerdmans Publishing Co., 1963. Used by permission.

Chapter 2: A Dangerous Doctrine?

1. White, John. *The Fight*, Downers Grove, IL: InterVarsity Press, ©1976.

Chapter 3: The Tyranny of the Law

1. Thomas, Major W. Ian. *The Saving Life of Christ*, Grand Rapids, MI: Zondervan, ©1961.
2. Luther, Martin. *Commentary on the Epistle to the Galatians*, Clark, ©1953.

Chapter 4: New Covenant Living

1. Packer, J.I. *Knowing God*, Downers Grove, IL: InterVarsity Press, ©1973.

Chapter 5: Grace and Habitual Sin—Part One

1. Stott, John. *The Epistles of John*, Grand Rapids, MI: William B. Eerdmans Publishing Co., ©1964.

2. Spurgeon, Charles. *The Epistles of John*, Grand Rapids, MI: Baker Book House, 1975.

Chapter 8: Grace and Self-Esteem

1. Stott, John. Taped message given at Cedar Campus, MI, 1987.
2. Stott, John. *Between Two Worlds*, Grand Rapids, MI: William B. Eerdmans Publishing Co., ©1982.
3. Phillips, J.B. *The Price of Success*, Wheaton, IL: Harold Shaw Publishers, 1984.
   Used by permission.
4. Lewis, C.S. *The Weight of Glory*, New York: Macmillan Co., ©1949.

Chapter 9: Grace and Physical Illness

1. Watson, David. *Fear No Evil*, Wheaton, IL: Harold Shaw Publishers, 1984.
   Used by permission.

Chapter 10: Grace and Truthful Speech

1. Taken from *Not Alone* by Keith and Gladys Hunt. Copyright ©1985 by Keith and Gladys Hunt. Used by permission of Zondervan Publishing House, Grand Rapids, MI.
2. Lewis, C.S. *The Weight of Glory*, New York: Macmillan Co., ©1949.

Chapter 11: Grace and Spiritual Ministry

1. Pippert, Becky. *Out of the Salt Shaker*, Downers Grove, IL: InterVarsity Press, ©1979.
2. Elliott, Elisabeth. *Shadow of the Almighty*, Grand Rapids, MI: Zondervan Publishing House, ©1958.

3. Stott, John. *God's New Society*, Downers Grove, IL: InterVarsity Press, ©1979.
4. Bunyan, John. *The Life of John Bunyan*, Grand Rapids, MI: Baker Book House, 1977.
5. Magnussen, Sally. *The Flying Scotsman*, London: Quartet Books, 1981.

Chapter 12: Grace and Financial blessing

1. Burkett, Larry. "A Principle Under Scrutiny," *How to Manage Your Money*, Issue 128, p. 2, July 15, 1988.

Chapter 13: Grace and Personal Freedom

1. Taken from *The Message of Galatians* by John R.W. Stott. ©1968 by John R.W. Stott. Used by permission of InterVarsity Press, P.O. Box 1400, Downers Grove, IL 60515.
2. Osbeck, Kenneth W. *101 Hymn Stories*, Grand Rapids, MI: Kregel Publications, ©1982.

Chapter 14: Keeping the Channels Open

1. Baxter, Richard. *The Reformed Pastor*, Portland, OR: Multnomah Press, ©1983.
2. Redpath, Alan. *My Most Memorable Encounters With God*, Wheaton, IL: Tyndale House Publishers, 1977.
3. From *The Pursuit of God*, by A.W. Tozer. Christian Publications, Camp Hill, PA. Used by permission.

This book was produced by the Christian Literature Crusade. We hope it has been helpful to you in living the Christian life. CLC is a literature mission with ministry in over 40 countries worldwide. If you would like to know more about us, or are interested in opportunities to serve with a faith mission, we invite you to write to:

Christian Literature Crusade
P.O. Box 1449
Fort Washington, PA 19034